LIVING WORD! LIVING WATER!

Adventurers

YEAR A

Susan Sayers
with Father Andrew Moore

TWENTY-THIRD PUBLICATIONS
BAYARD Mystic, CT 06355

YEAR A
Adventurers

First published in 1998 by
KEVIN MAYHEW LTD
Buxhall
Stowmarket
Suffolk IP14 3BW

North American copyright © 2000 Susan Sayers
Twenty-Third Publications/Bayard185 Willow Street
P.O. Box 180
Mystic, CT 06355
(860) 536-2611
(800) 321-0411

ISBN: 1-58595-097-1
Printed in U.S.A.

The other titles in the *Living Word! Living Water! Year A* series are

Complete Resource Book	ISBN 1-58595-094-7
Seekers	ISBN 1-58595-095-5
Explorers	ISBN 1-58595-096-3

Edited by Katherine Laidler
Illustrated by Fred Chevalier

Foreword

While many churches provide for the needs of the children, there is often an uncomfortable gap where young people are concerned. This is the age when deep questions are being asked, and it is essential that our young people find in their churches those who are going to listen and not be shocked; those who are willing to enter into real discussion and provide relevant and unsuffocating support during adolescence.

Many churches are well aware of the needs, but find it difficult to provide for them. They are concerned about this age group feeling too old for children's liturgy but not able to relate to what adults are doing in church. Sadly, the result is often an exodus of young people, just when their faith could be (and often is) taking off.

Not only do our young people need the Church, the Church badly needs its young people. Their insistence on rejecting every hint of hypocrisy, and their gift of presenting challenging ideas with wit and enthusiasm—these are good for everyone and vital for a healthy body of Christ.

This program aims to provide relevant and varied activities for young people which stimulate their thinking and encourage valuable discussion. Although some young people may be involved on the children's liturgy team, I am convinced that they need feeding at their own level as well.

The factfiles on each week's activity sheet can be collected into a book so that the course becomes a reference manual. It could also be used as an ongoing course for confirmation.

All the material in the book is copyright-free for non-commercial use.

SUSAN SAYERS
with Father Andrew Moore

This book is dedicated to my family and friends,
whose encouraging support has been wonderful,
and to all those whose good ideas are included here for others to share.

Acknowledgments

The Publishers wish to express their gratitude to the following for permission to use copyright material in this book:

GIA Publications Inc, 7404 S. Mason Avenue, Chicago, IL 60638, for verse 1 from *Heaven Shall Not Wait* by John L. Bell and Graham Maule, © Copyright 1987 WGRG and used by permission from the *Heaven Shall Not Wait* collection, and verse 1 of *Christ's is the World* by John L. Bell and Graham Maule, © Copyright 1989 WGRG and used by permission from the *Love From Below* collection.

EMI Christian Music Publishing, P.O. Box 5085, Brentwood, TN 37024, for the chorus from *Meekness and Majesty* by Graham Kendrick, © 1986 Kingsway's Thankyou Music; the chorus from *The Heart of Worship* by Matt Redman, © 1997 Kingsway's Thankyou Music. All rights in the Western Hemisphere administered by EMI Christian Music Publishing.

Integrity's Hosanna! Music, PO Box 16801, Mobile, AL 36616, for the chorus of *There is None Like You* by Lenny Leblanc, © 1991 Integrity's Hosanna! Music/ASCAP.

Contents

SPECIAL FEASTS

Christmas Day

Christmas Day is very much a time for all God's children to worship together, and I have not included separate ideas or activity sheets for the young people.

Use some of the All-age suggestions in the *Living Word! Living Water! Complete Resource Book,* or involve the young people in planning part of the service, and in the music group or choir, as servers, welcomers, collectors of the offering, decorating the church and so on.

Advent

First Sunday of Advent

Thought for the day

We are to wake up and make sure we stay ready for the second coming.

Readings

Isaiah 2:1–5
Romans 13:11–14
Matthew 24:37–44

Aim: To look at why we are to be ready and watchful.

Starter

Sit in a circle around a table or on the floor. Explain that you are going to give them a coded word and they have to try and crack the code. This is the code. For each letter you say something beginning with it—for S you might say, "So you have to watch carefully." For vowels you tap on the floor or table one, two, three, four or five times (for E you tap twice). The confusing thing is that you don't draw attention to either the speaking or the tapping, but to arranging some knives and forks in different and complex ways in front of you. This distracts them from seeing what is really important!

When you have made a word, tell them the word you have said, and then do it in code again (using different sentences). If no one guesses, try another word. If someone thinks they have cracked the code let them try doing a word themselves. If no one guesses the secret, give increasingly obvious clues until they do.

Teaching

Talk about how necessary it was to pay attention to the right things in order to crack the code. In our life there are lots of things we are pressured into thinking are important, and if we aren't careful we can end up giving our attention to them and ignoring what is really important.

Read Romans 13:11–14 together, to see what Paul has to say to help us in this. What kind of behavior in our society would Paul call "living in the darkness" How do they think we can live today "in the light"? (You can record their suggestions on a large sheet, placed under a table lamp, or they can use the activity sheet.)

Now look at what Jesus told us about the time when he will return to earth in glory (Matthew 24:37–44). Draw attention to what we don't know and what we do: no one will know the time or date in advance, but we do know that things will carry on as normal right up to when it happens. Show them a front door key and talk about burglar alarms. When is the best time for a burglar to be unnoticed? When the people in the house are too busy to check their doors and windows before they go out; when they're asleep; or when they're deeply into their favorite video.

Place the key on another sheet of paper, and record here their ideas on ways we can make sure we are not taken by surprise, totally unprepared.

Praying

Lord our God,
make us watchful and keep us faithful
as we wait for the coming of your Son our Lord;
that, when he appears,
he may not find us sleeping in sin
but active in his service
and joyful in his praise. Amen.

Activities

On the activity sheet there are guidelines for them to create a short piece of drama based on being prepared and active. They may like to share this with those in church.

Discussion starters

1. In what ways is the historical site of Jerusalem still a center of pilgrimage? Why are so many people drawn to it?

2. Why do you think the timing of the second coming is known only to God the Father? How might it affect us if we knew all the details in advance?

Notes

WHERE ARE YOU?

LIVING IN THE LIGHT

LIVING IN THE DARKNESS

Romans 13 : 11–14

THE SECOND COMING OF JESUS

WHAT WE DO KNOW	WHAT WE DON'T KNOW

ADVENT

I KNOW ADVENT MEANS 'COMING'. WHAT OR WHO IS COMING?

Jesus.

BUT HE CAME 2000 YEARS AGO, DIDN'T HE?

Yes. We are looking back to that and getting ready to welcome him again.

I THOUGHT HE WAS KILLED ON A CROSS AGES AGO?

He was. But he came back to life and is still alive now. He's alive forever.

WILL HE COME BACK TO EARTH ONE DAY THEN?

Yes! That's the other coming we're getting ready for.

DRAMA

SITUATION — GETTING READY FOR MOVING HOUSE, WITH THE FAMILY PACKING. THE MOVING VAN IS DUE AFTER LUNCH.

PROBLEM — DOORBELL RINGS — THE MOVING VAN HAS ARRIVED AT 9 AM — THEY'D GOT THE TIME WRONG.

RESULT — PANIC !!!

ALL: BE READY !

LORD OUR GOD,
MAKE US WATCHFUL AND KEEP US FAITHFUL
AS WE WAIT FOR THE COMING
OF YOUR SON OUR LORD;
THAT, WHEN HE APPEARS,
HE MAY NOT FIND US SLEEPING IN SIN
BUT ACTIVE IN HIS SERVICE
AND JOYFUL IN HIS PRAISE.
— AMEN —

Second Sunday of Advent

Thought for the day
Get the road ready for the Lord!

Readings
Isaiah 11:1–10
Romans 15:4–9
Matthew 3:1–12

Aim: To see the link between the prophecies and John the Baptist's message.

Starter
Give out road maps and work out the most direct route from one place to another, noting any sections of the route where there may be problems or hold-ups.

Teaching
Show them a picture of a tree chopped down with only the stump still standing. Explain how the people of Israel had been taken into exile, and must have felt as though their nation was like this tree. Now read the passage from Isaiah and, as it is read, draw a shoot growing from the tree stump. Talk about how the people hearing this prophecy might have felt; the possibility of real hope because of God's faithfulness to them.

Can they give a name to the promised fresh shoot from the stump of Jesse? Help them to see how Jesus was the fulfillment of the prophecy.

Now read Matthew 3:1–12, listening for another prophecy being fulfilled, linked with the one we have heard. Talk about what the prophecy was and how it was fulfilled. What do they think John meant by making the road ready? They can look at what John encouraged his listeners to do in order to be ready. Did they spot another prophecy? This one is given by John the Baptist. Find it (it's in verses 11–12) and talk about whether it has yet been fulfilled.

Praying
Lord God of Israel, we praise you.
Only you can work miracles.
We will always praise your glorious name.
Let your glory be seen everywhere on earth. Amen.
(From Psalm 72)

Activities
The activity sheet helps them to plot the prophecies and their fulfillment, and to think of areas in their own lives which need making ready.

Discussion starters
1. Does our church's outreach reflect a belief that God's good news is for all, or for the few who "do it our way"?
2. Is Isaiah's righteous, just and compassionate living realistic, or simply a pipe-dream which can disillusion us?

Notes

Third Sunday of Advent

Thought for the day

Great expectations. Jesus fulfills the great statements of prophecy.

Readings

Isaiah 35:1–6, 10
James 5:7–10
Matthew 11:2–11

Aim: To recognize that God sometimes takes us by surprise, especially when our idea of him has been too narrow.

Starter

Play *Twister,* where you have to be quite flexible to bend into the right positions. Or try some simple yoga exercises designed to make you flexible and supple.

Teaching

It isn't only our bodies which can be stiff and unbending. Spiritually we also need to be flexible, so we're ready to see God at work in ways we might not expect.

Read the Isaiah passage, making note of the "marks of the kingdom" in the prophecy. Then go through the list, thinking of how Jesus behaved when he lived on earth many years after Isaiah's prophecy. Check off the things Jesus fulfilled. Now read the gospel, as far as verse three. Why did John have these doubts, when it was John who had prepared the way for Jesus' coming?

Discuss their ideas, and refer to last week's reading—Matthew 3:12—to see what kind of Messiah John seems to have been expecting. How might that expectation have caused the doubts to come into his mind? Carry on reading today's Gospel to see how Jesus replied to John.

Praying

My soul glorifies the Lord
and my spirit rejoices
in God my Savior…
for the Mighty One has done
great things for me—
holy is his Name!

(From Mary's song)

Activities

In Advent we are getting ourselves into a state of readiness, and that means being flexible. Some of the group may enjoy putting some flexible exercises to a song about God being greater than we can ever imagine—for example, *Lord Jesus Christ.* The activity sheet also encourages some flexible thinking.

Discussion starters

1. Look at the "checklist" of Isaiah 35:1–6, 10. What kind of kingdom does this suggest, and how does it differ from what John the Baptist was preaching in last Sunday's gospel passage (Matthew 3:1–12)?

2. How do we sometimes limit God by our narrow expectations?

Notes

GOD of SURPRISES

WHAT DOES 'MESSIAH' MEAN?

'Messiah' or 'Christ' was the one God would send to save his people. The Jewish people were waiting for him to come.

WAS JOHN THE BAPTIST EXPECTING HIM TOO?

Yes.

SO WHY DIDN'T HE KNOW JESUS WAS THIS CHRIST?

Mostly he did know. But a bit of him wasn't sure because he was behaving more as a friend of sinners than a judge.

IS THIS A STAIRCASE FROM ABOVE OR UNDERNEATH?

IS THIS TWO PEOPLE OR A CANDLESTICK?

THINGS AREN'T ALWAYS WHAT THEY SEEM

IS THIS A PERSON ON A BIKE OR A FRIED EGG ON A SAUSAGE?

IS THIS A SAD BALD BEARDED MAN OR A HAPPY BOY?

HOW DID JESUS' MINISTRY FIT IN WITH THE PROPHECIES ABOUT THE MESSIAH, OR CHRIST?

- FROM MARY'S SONG -
MY SOUL GLORIFIES THE LORD AND MY SPIRIT REJOICES IN GOD MY SAVIOUR ...
FOR THE MIGHTY ONE HAS DONE GREAT THINGS FOR ME.
HOLY IS HIS NAME!

WHAT WAS JOHN THE BAPTIST WONDERING AS HE SAT IN PRISON?

Fourth Sunday of Advent

Thought for the day

Through the willing participation of Mary and Joseph, God is poised to come among his people as their Savior.

Readings

Isaiah 7:10–14
Romans 1:1–7
Matthew 1:18–24

Aim: To look at the way God enjoys cooperating with us.

Starter

Body shapes. The whole group cooperates to create a shape which the leader calls out. Then they change to another shape. Shape ideas: Make yourselves into a comb/a centipede/a mug/an electric plug.

Teaching

Talk about the way we needed to cooperate to create those amazing shapes out of bodies. God likes to cooperate with his people to bring about all kinds of good; today we are going to look at how Joseph and Mary cooperated with God so that his plan to save us could take place.

Read the Isaiah passage together, and draw attention to the hopes for rescue and the signs which Matthew later picked up as he looked at Jesus' birth. Now read the first part of the gospel, up to the point that Joseph has decided the most honorable way to act in the circumstances. Ask them to restate this situation in their own language, and record this on a chart. Point out that, for an honorable man of that time, there was not a viable alternative to divorce; the problem for Joseph was whether to make a great fuss of Mary's assumed unfaithfulness and have her publicly stoned, in order to clear his own name, or whether to take the braver step of divorcing her quietly, without making any accusations or voicing his righteous indignation.

Then read the rest of the gospel, and together try to build up a picture of Joseph going to bed worried by what Mary has told him and the effect of the dream on him.

Praying

Lord Jesus Christ,
you have no body on earth but ours,
no hands but ours,
no feet but ours.
Ours are the eyes through which
your compassion must look out on the world.
Ours are the feet by which
you may still go about doing good.
Ours are the hands with which
you bless people now.
Bless our minds and bodies,
that we may be a blessing to others.

(Based on a prayer of St. Teresa of Avila)

Activities

On the activity sheet there are some examples of people working in cooperation with God, which can lead into discussion about their own willingness to be available to God's possibilities, both individually and as a church.

Discussion starters

1. What methods have you noticed God using to alert people to repentance or to a new and better way of dealing with a difficult situation?

2. How can the transcendent God work in partnership with ordinary people? Where have you seen this happening?

Notes

WORKING WITH GOD

HOW COME GOD NEEDS OUR HELP? I THOUGHT HE COULD DO EVERYTHING?

He can. But because he loves us, he made us able to have a relationship with him and share in his work.

SUPPOSE WE DO IT WRONG?

God certainly takes risks. But he gives us lots of help and support.

COULD I HELP, THEN? I'D LIKE TO WORK WITH A STAR-MAKER.

You can, then. Just offer your services and God will take you up on your offer.

WHAT ARE WE DOING?

WHAT CAN WE DO?

LORD JESUS CHRIST,
YOU HAVE NO BODY ON EARTH BUT OURS,
NO HANDS BUT OURS,
NO FEET BUT OURS.
OURS ARE THE EYES THROUGH WHICH
YOUR COMPASSION MUST LOOK OUT ON THE WORLD.
OURS ARE THE FEET BY WHICH
YOU MAY STILL GO ABOUT DOING GOOD.
OURS ARE THE HANDS WITH WHICH
YOU BLESS PEOPLE NOW.
BLESS OUR MINDS AND BODIES,
THAT WE MAY BE A BLESSING TO OTHERS.

First Sunday After Christmas: The Holy Family

Thought for the day

Jesus, the expression of God's love, lives as a vulnerable boy in the real and dangerous world we all inhabit.

Reflection on the readings

Sirach 3:2–6, 12–14
Colossians 3:12–21
Matthew 2:13–15, 19–23

Aim: To understand the risk God was prepared to take in coming to save us.

Starter

Rescue! Play this game in which someone needs rescuing from a magic castle. (This is a chair with a length of rope on the floor encircling it.) The only way to break the evil magic is to get the key which fits the lock. (This is a rectangular card from which a key shape has been cut. The key has been cut into several pieces. When the group has collected all the pieces the completed key should fit the card shape.) Hide the pieces around the building, and pass a dice around the group. When anyone throws a six they can go hunting for a piece of the key.

Teaching

We know that God loves his people and really wants to look after them and save them. But, bearing in mind that we were all created with free will—we are free to choose either good or evil—what are the risks involved if God comes in person to save the world? Make a note of their ideas.

Now read today's gospel, looking out for the risks and dangers. Make a note of these too. Through Joseph and Mary working with God, the baby is kept safe, at least for the moment. What happened when he grew up? Was the risk worth taking if Jesus was going to end up being put to death? Again, make a note of their ideas.

The risks were worth taking because it meant that through becoming human and sharing human experiences, Jesus could really help us and save us, even though it meant that he had to suffer death in the process.

Praying

Thank you, Lord Jesus,
for coming to share our human lives.
Dying, you destroyed our death.
Rising, you restored our life.
Lord Jesus, come again in glory.

Activities

On the activity sheet there is a map which traces the journey taken to Egypt and back to Nazareth, and they can look up the references Matthew uses to show the Jewish readers how Jesus was fulfilling their ancient prophecies. These references will be needed for them to complete a crossword puzzle.

Discussion starters

1. From the reading of today's gospel, what kind of person does Joseph seem to be, and what can we learn from him that might help us in dealing with crises in our own lives?

2. What was the advantage of Jesus being born as a human baby, rather than appearing as an adult to save the world?

Notes

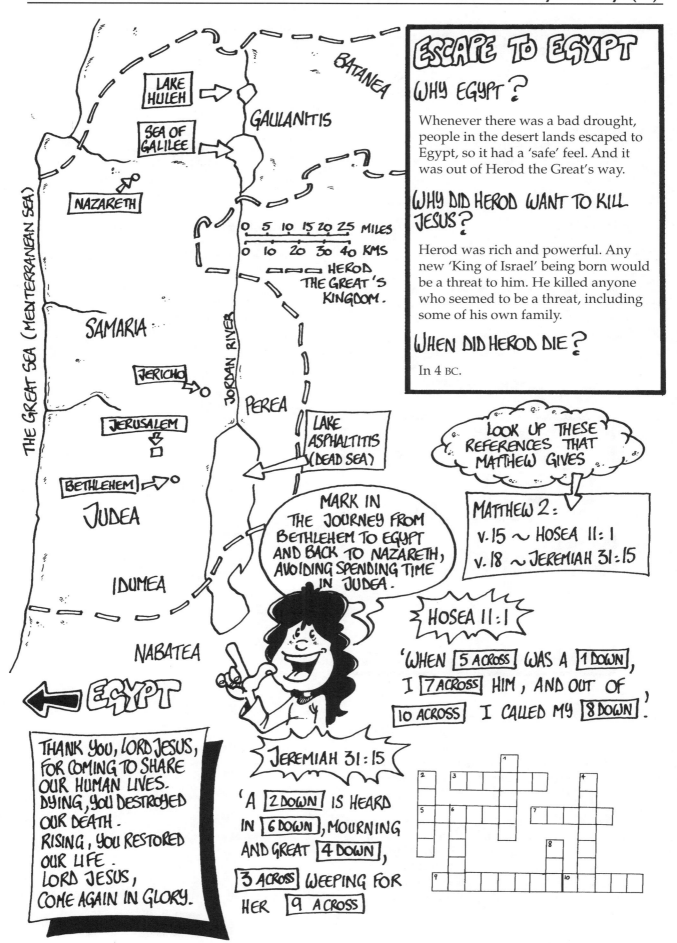

ESCAPE TO EGYPT

WHY EGYPT?

Whenever there was a bad drought, people in the desert lands escaped to Egypt, so it had a 'safe' feel. And it was out of Herod the Great's way.

WHY DID HEROD WANT TO KILL JESUS?

Herod was rich and powerful. Any new 'King of Israel' being born would be a threat to him. He killed anyone who seemed to be a threat, including some of his own family.

WHEN DID HEROD DIE?

In 4 BC.

LOOK UP THESE REFERENCES THAT MATTHEW GIVES

MATTHEW 2:
v.15 ~ HOSEA 11:1
v.18 ~ JEREMIAH 31:15

MARK IN THE JOURNEY FROM BETHLEHEM TO EGYPT AND BACK TO NAZARETH, AVOIDING SPENDING TIME IN JUDEA.

HOSEA 11:1

'WHEN [5 ACROSS] WAS A [1 DOWN], I [7 ACROSS] HIM, AND OUT OF [10 ACROSS] I CALLED MY [8 DOWN].'

JEREMIAH 31:15

'A [2 DOWN] IS HEARD IN [6 DOWN], MOURNING AND GREAT [4 DOWN], [3 ACROSS] WEEPING FOR HER [9 ACROSS]'

THANK YOU, LORD JESUS, FOR COMING TO SHARE OUR HUMAN LIVES. DYING, YOU DESTROYED OUR DEATH. RISING, YOU RESTORED OUR LIFE. LORD JESUS, COME AGAIN IN GLORY.

Second Sunday After Christmas

Thought for the day

The grace and truth revealed in Jesus show God's freely given love; through Jesus, God pours out his blessings on us and gives us real freedom.

Readings

Sirach 24:1–2, 8–12
Ephesians 1:3–6, 15–18
John 1:1–18

Aim: To explore the nature of Jesus as the eternal Word.

Starter

One person in the group is given a chart to follow like the one following. This person gives the instructions out so that eventually everyone is arranged on chairs in the way shown on the chart.

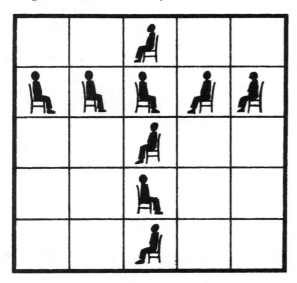

Teaching

Discuss the impressive effect of the spoken instructions. Words spoken can bring creative things about. An orchestra or band can play out the ideas in the composer's mind. A book (show some examples) can take you off to other countries or other ages in your mind, just through the words on the pages. Words have power.

Now read John 1:1–18, checking for meaning as you go along. Link the first three verses with the first few verses of Genesis and help them see the connections. (Pick up on the darkness in which the loving Word brings light; how is that true of both passages?) Draw their thinking together in the last verse: the Son has shown us what God is like. Explain that the Greek word for "word" (logos) meant any kind of communication, much as we might "say it with flowers" or describe someone's actions as "speaking volumes."

Praying

Word of the Father,
now in flesh appearing.
O come, let us adore him,
Christ the Lord. Amen.

Activities

The activity sheet has space to record some of the links between Genesis and John's introduction, and helps them explore the meaning of Jesus as the Word of God.

Discussion starters

1. What has or would it cost you to receive Jesus into your daily living, your work, leisure, politics, finances and popularity?

2. Is it worth it?

Notes

The Epiphany of the Lord

Thought for the day

Jesus, the hope of the nations, is shown to the world.

Readings

Isaiah 60:1–6
Ephesians 3:2–3, 5–6
Matthew 2:1–12

Aim: To understand how the wise men's visit symbolizes all the nations coming to worship God.

Starter

A quest for the truth. As with the younger group, this involves having an identity fixed on your back. You can ask everyone else questions to discover your identity but they can only answer yes or no. Instead of pictures have names of famous people for this group.

Teaching

Read the Matthew passage for today, with different people taking the parts. Point out that the wise men were also involved with a quest for the truth. Use the activity sheet to jot down all the things that helped them in their quest and all the things which threatened to make it fail. Also think about what made them set off on such a journey in the first place.

Now look at part of the Isaiah prophecy (Isaiah 60:1–4). How do the wise men fit in with this? Help them to see how they are in a way representing all the nations: God's salvation is not only for the nations of Israel but for the whole world.

Praying

Have a world map spread out on the floor. As you play some quiet music or sing a worship song or a Taizé chant, one by one the members of the group light candles in holders and place them on various parts of the world.

Activities

Make a collage for prayer which can be displayed in church or in the hall. Have a selection of newspaper pictures and stories showing some of the areas of need and evil in our world. Arrange them around a central picture (perhaps from a Christmas card) showing the wise men offering their gifts. Have the words from Isaiah 60:1–4 written on the collage.

Discussion starters

1. Why did Herod find the prophesied birth threatening, while the magi were excited enough to travel many miles to see this child?

2. The Celtic Christians were very aware that the journey is, in a way, the destination. How is this true?

Notes

22

THE QUEST

WISE MEN FROM THE EAST COME TO FIND JESUS

EPIPHANY

WHAT DOES 'EPIPHANY' MEAN?

It comes from Greek and it means being shown, or revealed, or manifested.

WHO WAS BEING REVEALED?

Jesus was being revealed to the Gentiles of other countries.

WHAT IS A GENTILE?

Someone who is not Jewish.

WHAT WAS THE STAR THEY SAW?

Some people think it was a comet, but others think it was two of the planets (Saturn and Jupiter) which were very close at that time.

WHAT HELPED THEM TO FIND HIM?

WHAT THREATENED TO MAKE IT FAIL?

WHY DID THEY SET OFF ON SUCH A JOURNEY?

'ALL NATIONS WILL COME AND BOW DOWN BEFORE ME.' ISAIAH 66.23

TRADITIONALLY, THE GIFTS HAVE COME TO MEAN THIS:

GOLD - A SIGN OF KINGSHIP AND PURITY OF CHARACTER

FRANKINCENSE A SIGN OF PRAYER AND WORSHIP TO GOD

MYRRH - A SIGN OF SUFFERING AND HUMAN DEATH

PRAYER FOR THE WORLD

LORD JESUS CHRIST SON OF THE LIVING GOD HAVE MERCY ON US.

The Baptism of the Lord

Thought for the day

As Jesus is baptized, the Spirit of God rests visibly on him, marking him out as the One who will save his people.

Readings

Isaiah 42:1–4, 6–7
Acts 10:34–38
Matthew 3:13–17

Aim: To see Jesus gradually being revealed as the fulfillment of God's promises.

Starter

Jigsaw puzzles. These can be done on their own or in pairs, or in a larger group, without the picture to help, so that the understanding of the picture gradually becomes apparent.

Teaching

Start by reading the prophecy from Isaiah, asking them to think of who it reminds them of. (Whoever the prophet was referring to at the time, Jesus certainly saw it as fitting in exactly with his own role.)

Take particular note of the opening verses, and then read Matthew's account of Jesus' Baptism, listening for any echoes of the Isaiah passage. They are now getting an idea of what it was like for the Jewish people to hear and read Matthew's gospel—they would pick up on familiar passages from Scripture which would help them to understand the way Jesus fulfilled the old prophecies. They could begin to see God's plan taking shape through history, and everything coming together in Jesus of Nazareth.

Praying

Take my life and let it be
consecrated, Lord, to thee.
Take my moments and my days,
let them flow in endless praise. Amen.

Activities

The activity sheet helps them explore Peter's understanding of Jesus' baptism, and their own ideas. There is also a short sketch which can be used in church, or as a way in to discussion about having our spiritual eyes open.

Discussion starters

1. What links are there between the Isaiah passage and the subsequent ministry of Jesus?
2. How does Peter explain what happened at Jesus' Baptism (Acts 10:38)? What is the significance of "anointing"?

Notes

TO SEE OR NOT TO SEE

Set up an optician (white-coated) with examination chair facing the audience. Optician has a flashlight, and mimes giving the eye examination. The audience see the words up behind the client.

Optician   Ah, good afternoon, madam. If you'd like to sit down here . . .

Client   Oh, thanks. I hope this won't take too long. I'm late already.

Optician   Just read me the letters on the board, madam.

Client   J, E, S, U, S / I, S / T, H, E / O, N, E / W, E / A, R, E / W, A, I, T, I, N, G / F, O, R.

Optician   Excellent sight, madam! Every letter clear to the very small print at the bottom.

Client   Can I go now, then?

Optician   What about the message, though? Can you read the message?

Client   Message – what message?

Optician   The one staring you in the eye, madam. You can see it clearly enough.

Client   No, I can't see any message. Does that mean I need glasses?

Optician   *(writing on her record card)* Physical sight: perfect. Spiritual sight: nil.

THE BAPTISM OF JESUS

IF YOU WERE JEWISH, WOULD YOU HAVE BEEN EXPECTING THE MESSIAH TO COME?

Yes. And you would pray for it every day.

SO IT MUST HAVE BEEN GREAT TO BE LIVING WHEN HE ACTUALLY CAME? For some, yes. But others didn't recognize him.

WHY NOT?

We tend to see what we're expecting, and Jesus wasn't the kind of warrior king they thought Messiah would be.

BUT JESUS FITS ISAIAH'S IDEA VERY CLOSELY.

Yes. But there is spiritual blindness as well as physical blindness.

JESUS IS THE ONE WE ARE WAITING FOR

READ ACTS 10:34-38

WHAT DOES PETER SAY HAPPENED TO JESUS?

ACTS 10:38

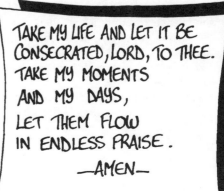

TAKE MY LIFE AND LET IT BE CONSECRATED, LORD, TO THEE. TAKE MY MOMENTS AND MY DAYS, LET THEM FLOW IN ENDLESS PRAISE.

—AMEN—

Lent

First Sunday of Lent

Thought for the day

Jesus knows all about temptation; and he can deal with our sin.

Readings

Genesis 2:7–9; 3:1–7
Romans 5:12–19
Matthew 4:1–11

Aim: To explore the way Jesus is seen as the second Adam.

Starter

Reversals. In pairs, work out a simple sequence of actions both the right way around and in reverse—for example, walking to post a letter; opening a present and being pleased with it; hammering a nail and hitting your thumb; packing a suitcase. These can be written on cards and given out to the pairs who work on them and perform them to the group in the reverse way first, seeing if people can guess from the reversal what the real action is before it is acted out.

Teaching

Today we are going to look at the greatest reversal of all time. Begin with the Genesis reading, encouraging different people to take the speaking parts, but as always being sensitive to readers who lack confidence or fluency. Try to get at the real sin of disobedience to God, and explain that Adam and Eve are the archetypal human beings, blowing it as they succumb to temptation in their weakness. We fail. We mess things up. We cannot put things right by ourselves.

Now read Romans 5, verses 17 and 19. This whole passage is so dense that I suggest you only look at these two verses which focus on the link between Adam and Jesus and the reversal of humanity's disobedience through Jesus' total and loving obedience. Talk about how Jesus showed that obedience, both in his life and his death, and how he did for us what we could never do for ourselves, purely out of love for us.

Finally look at Matthew's account of Jesus' temptations, to see his obedience in action right at the beginning of his ministry.

Praying

O loving wisdom of our God!
when all was sin and shame
a second Adam to the fight
and to the rescue came.
Oh wisest love! that flesh and blood,
which did in Adam fail,
should strive afresh against the foe,
should strive and should prevail.
Praise to the Holiest in the height,
and in the depth be praise;
in all his words most wonderful,
most sure in all his ways.

Activities

On the activity sheet there is a temptation sketch and some suggestions for recognizing temptation and working in God's strength to resist it. There is also an Adam/Jesus factfile to fill in. It is important that they understand the difference between temptation and sin, and that they are made aware of the reality and power of temptation and so the need to wear God's "armor."

Discussion starters

1. Can we help one another more to resist temptation or is this always a battle we have to fight on our own?

2. How are Adam and Jesus similar, and how are they different?

Notes

Mom *(calls)* Hey, Mark, can you come here a sec?

Tempter *(whispers)* Pretend you haven't heard!

Mark But I did. And she needs me to help her.

Tempter And you've just put your feet up.

Mark That's true. It's been quite a day and I need a bit of a rest before tonight.

Mom Mark! Did you hear, love?

Mark But I expect she's tired as well. And, like I said, she needs my help.

Tempter Well, tell her you're doing your homework. Then she won't know you're being lazy. She'll think you're being hardworking. *And* you won't have to get up out of that comfortable chair.

Mark But it isn't true, is it? I'm *not* doing my homework – I'm loafing here and showing her I don't want to help. I'm telling her I don't care.

(He gets up and goes to the kitchen)

Mark Yes, Mom? What did you want?

Mom Oh, there you are, Mark. Thanks for helping, love. I know you're tired and I really appreciate it.

Tempter Drat! 4-3 to him! Just wait till next time. I'll try less 'comfort zone' and more 'right things for the wrong reasons'. That should do it!

TEMPTATION

WHAT WERE ADAM AND EVE TEMPTED TO DO?

They were tempted to disobey God. That's the basic point of all sin.

SO IT WASN'T ANYTHING TO DO WITH SEX OR APPLES? Not really.

Their sin was to go against what God had told them, and that was disobedience.

WHY IS IT SO HARD TO RESIST TEMPTATION? Because we naturally want to be self-centered, not loving.

IS IT WORTH FIGHTING TEMPTATION?

Yes! God gives us the strength and protection we need, and when we live loving lives we are at peace with ourselves and fulfilled.

IF YOU FIND YOURSELF WANTING TO SIN, IS THAT JUST AS MUCH WRONG AS IF YOU ACTUALLY DO IT?

NO. BEING TEMPTED ISN'T A SIN. 'YOU CAN'T STOP A BIRD FLYING INTO YOUR HAIR, BUT YOU CAN STOP IT MAKING ITS NEST THERE!'

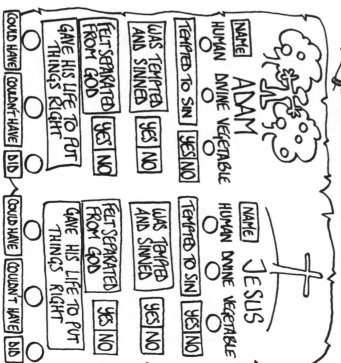

O LOVING WISDOM OF OUR GOD!
WHEN ALL WAS SIN AND SHAME
A SECOND ADAM TO THE FIGHT
AND TO THE RESCUE CAME.
O WISEST LOVE! THAT FLESH AND BLOOD,
WHICH DID IN ADAM FAIL,
SHOULD STRIVE AFRESH AGAINST THE FOE,
SHOULD STRIVE AND SHOULD PREVAIL.
PRAISE TO THE HOLIEST IN THE HEIGHT,
AND IN THE DEPTH BE PRAISE;
IN ALL HIS WORDS MOST WONDERFUL,
MOST SURE IN ALL HIS WAYS.

Second Sunday of Lent

Thought for the day

The disciples witness the glory of God revealed in Jesus. It is a glimpse of the glory which will be the great hope for all nations of the world.

Readings

Genesis 12:1–4
2 Timothy 1:8–10
Matthew 17:1–9

Aim: To see how the Transfiguration links with Abraham, Moses and Elijah.

Starter

Show these pictures (or others of your own) which show only a small section of the complete object, and try to work out what the full pictures are.

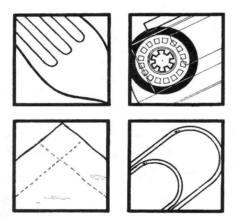

Teaching

Have a speech bubble on which is written God's call and promise to Abram. Look at this first, noticing how Abram is called out of where he is living to go forward in God's company into the unknown, sustained by the promise. Now look at the gospel reading. In another speech bubble write what the disciples heard God saying, and draw attention to the way Abram's faithful listening enabled much to happen in his life; the disciples' faithful listening will also strengthen and uphold them through the times of suffering ahead.

Why were Moses and Elijah there at the Transfiguration? (They may need you to give a thumbnail sketch of the role of Moses and Elijah.) Help them to see that they represent the authority of the Law and the prophets. See how this links in with the authority of God's words to Abram, and his words on the mountain, declaring to the disciples who Jesus is.

Praying

O worship the Lord in the beauty of holiness;
bow down before him, his glory proclaim;
with gold of obedience and incense of lowliness,
kneel and adore him: the Lord is his name.

Activities

On the activity sheet there are suggestions to start them off in a Peter, James and John role-play conversation, a mountaintop comparison and some thoughts to get them seeing the value and the dangers of mountaintop experiences.

Discussion starters

1. Do we hit the right balance in our prayer and public worship between intimate friendship and awe in the presence of the almighty God?

2. Do we want to cling on to the "mountain experiences" rather than accompany the living Jesus down to the demands of life in the valley?

Notes

WHAT'S THE SAME?

MOSES — EXODUS 24 12-18

2 MOUNTAINS

MATTHEW 17 1-9 — JESUS — WHAT'S DIFFERENT?

A MOUNTAINTOP EXPERIENCE

WHAT HAPPENED?
Jesus took his friends up a mountain.

WHICH FRIENDS?
Peter, James and John.

WHAT DID THEY SEE?
Jesus started praying and they saw his glory – God's glory. He was talking with Moses and Elijah.

WERE THEY FRIGHTENED?
Yes, at first.

WHY DID JESUS SHOW HIS GLORY LIKE THAT?
It would help them cope with the crucifixion and eventually understand who Jesus was.

PETER   JAMES   JOHN

O WORSHIP THE LORD
IN THE BEAUTY OF HOLINESS;
BOW DOWN BEFORE HIM,
HIS GLORY PROCLAIM;
WITH GOLD OF OBEDIENCE
AND INCENSE OF LOWLINESS,
KNEEL AND ADORE HIM:
THE LORD IS HIS NAME.

GET INTO 3'S AS PETER, JAMES AND JOHN AND TALK ABOUT WHAT HAPPENED ...

Third Sunday of Lent

Thought for the day

God both knows us completely and loves us completely; meeting us where we are, he provides us with living water, to satisfy all our needs.

Readings

Exodus 17:3–7
Romans 5:1–2, 5–8
John 4:5–42

Aim: To explore the meaning and significance of "living water."

Starter

Play *hoop-la*, using bottles of different spring water. If you don't have any small hoops, cut cross-sections from a large plastic bottle. This game is about aiming for water, and how our aim often falls short or wide of the mark.

Teaching

Cut out an arrow from thin card and fix it with a split pin on to the background as shown in this illustration:

Read the Exodus passage together, listening out for why the people were grumbling. Which way were they facing? (They were looking back to the *past* in Egypt, rather than seeing that God was with them in the present, leading them into the *future*.) What about Moses? (He was looking at God in the *present*, and helped the people to recognize this too. Now they could look confidently to the *future* in God's company.)

Then look at the gospel—John 4:5–42. How was the woman still imprisoned by the past? (Her own relationships; society's attitude; religious and national traditions and expectations.) How is Jesus like clear running water for her? (Look at the cleansing, refreshing and life-giving properties of water and see how these are also spiritual qualities.)

Praying

River, wash over me,
cleanse me and make me new.
Bathe me, refresh me and fill me anew.
River, wash over me. Amen.

Activities

On the activity sheet there are various references to help them unpack the meaning and significance of Jesus as "living water," and outlets of world and personal needs which they can fill in as prayer concerns.

Discussion starters

1. What kind of sources do we tend to use and rely on rather than God's living water? Why?

2. What does Jesus' conversation with the Samaritan woman teach us about our dealings as Christians with other people?

Notes

Fourth Sunday of Lent

Thought for the day
Jesus gives sight to the man born blind and exposes the blindness of those who claim to see.

Readings
1 Samuel 16:1, 6–7, 10–13
Ephesians 5:8–14
John 9:1–41

Aim: To explore the issue of spiritual sight and blindness.

Starter
Provide a selection of magazines and newspaper supplements, glue and scissors. Write certain characteristics on separate sheets of paper and ask everyone to choose images which seem to go with the characteristics. Here are some ideas: relaxed, ambitious, violent, dangerous, important, stressed.

Teaching
Look at the different collections of images and talk about how we make judgments based on what people look and dress like. Talk about dressing to impress, and the reasons we would choose particular clothes and refuse to wear others. We are constantly being told that our image is very important. Today we hear a rather different message: people look at the outward appearance but God looks at the heart.

Read the passage from 1 Samuel 16, seeing how people were just the same thousands of years ago—still tending to judge from appearances. Then read from Ephesians, which suggests that if we are "dressed" in God's love it should really show in our attitudes and relationships; that is what walking by the light means. Our behavior should be consistent with what we claim to believe.

Now read the gospel, with different voices for the characters and narrator, thinking as you read, "Who is blind in this story?" Talk about how the blind man is given both physical and spiritual sight, and how the Pharisees are spiritually blind, even though physically sighted.

Praying
God be in my head and in my understanding.
God be in my eyes and in my looking.
God be in my mouth and in my speaking.
God be in my heart and in my thinking.
God be at my end and at my departing.

(Book of Hours, 1514)

Activities
There is a short sketch which explores the way we often make wrong judgments based on appearance, and a look at what is sight and what is blindness, spiritually speaking.

Discussion starters
1. Does the world's habit of looking at the outward appearance rub off on Christians so that even those in the church do it?

2. In what ways are the sighted Pharisees "blind" and the blind man sighted?

Notes

SEEING ISN'T ALL EYE WORK

Doris	Our new priest won't be any good, you know.
George	Won't he, Doris? Why's that?
Doris	Well, you've only got to look at him.
George	He looks fairly normal to me – two legs, two eyes, a mouth, two ears – that sort of thing.
Doris	That's just it! His ears!
George	What – stick out a bit, do they? Can't say I'd . . .
Doris	Pierced! His left ear. It's pierced. And his right eyebrow. He must be up to no good, I'm telling you.
George	But you've had your ears pierced, Doris. I bought you those very expensive hanging pearl ones for your last birthday, remember?
Doris	Oh, George, that's *quite* different! I'm a woman. Women are allowed to have their ears pierced.
George	Who says? I don't recall reading anything about it in the Good Book. 'If thou art not a woman then shalt thou never pierce thy left ear nor thy right eyebrow.'
Doris	You mark my words – he'll be rude and a young thug. He won't even notice we've come to Mass.
Priest	Ah, good morning, you two! Doris, isn't it? Doris Crab. And you must be George. It was good to see you both at Mass – it's wonderful to see the established members of the church welcoming those from the new housing estate.
Doris	Oh . . . er . . . yes, we're the Crabs. Welcome to All Saints.

SIGHT AND BLINDNESS

WHO COULD SEE?

The man born blind. Jesus healed his physical sight and opened his eyes in another way, too.

WHAT WAY?

It helped him to see that the one who had healed him was God's Son.

WHO WAS BLIND, THEN?

The Pharisees. They could see fine, physically, but spiritually their eyes were shut tight so they couldn't see that Jesus was Messiah.

GOD BE IN MY HEAD AND IN MY UNDERSTANDING.
GOD BE IN MY EYES AND IN MY LOOKING.
GOD BE IN MY MOUTH AND IN MY SPEAKING.
GOD BE IN MY HEART AND IN MY THINKING.
GOD BE AT MY END AND AT MY DEPARTING.

(– BOOK OF HOURS, 1514 –)

SPEAKING SPIRITUALLY...

WHAT DOES IT MEAN TO 'SEE'?

AND WHAT DOES IT MEAN TO BE 'BLIND'?

Fifth Sunday of Lent

Thought for the day

Jesus is the resurrection and the life. He can transform death and despair, in any form, into life and hope.

Readings

Ezekiel 37:12–14
Romans 8:8–11
John 11:1–45

Aim: To explore the ways in which Jesus is the resurrection and the life.

Starter

Use a paper kit for constructing a skeleton, or make a simplified home-made one from thin card.

Teaching

First explain that the people of Israel were living in exile, and felt there was no hope for them when Ezekiel had his vision of people being raised from their graves. Then read the Old Testament passage. What would this image have said to the people, bearing in mind where they were coming from? Bring out the message of hope and God's capacity for transforming even the most hopeless situation.

What about the dead situations in our world and in our own life? Write some of these down on paper and then read the story of Lazarus. Several people can take part in this reading, or it could be acted out. What has it to say about some of the situations you wrote down? What does it tell us about Jesus and who he is?

Praying

Out of the depths have I called to you, O Lord:
Lord, hear my voice.
If you, Lord, should note what we do wrong:
who then, O Lord, could stand?

But there is forgiveness with you:
so that you shall be revered.
I wait for the Lord, my soul waits for him:
and in his word is my hope. Amen.

(From Psalm 130)

Activities

On the activity sheet there are various pictures used by the prophets to explain God's message which can be matched with the meanings. These can be used as discussion starters for opening up their receptiveness to the different ways God speaks to us. There is space for them to explore and note the ideas that come from reading the story of Lazarus, from various different viewpoints.

Discussion starters

1. How would the image of bodies raised from their graves help the exiled people Ezekiel was called to speak to?

2. Compare the responses of Martha and Mary and Thomas. What do we learn about the strengths and weaknesses of each?

Notes

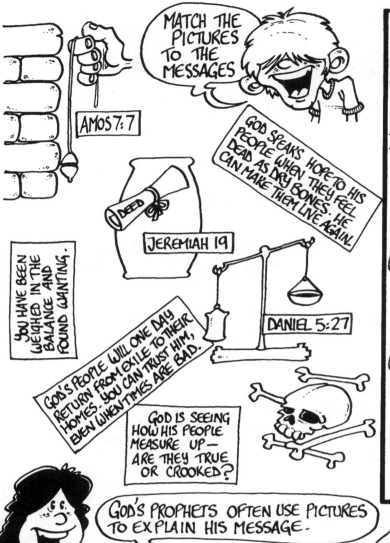

MATCH THE PICTURES TO THE MESSAGES

AMOS 7:7

GOD SPEAKS HOPE TO HIS PEOPLE WHEN THEY FEEL DEAD AS DRY BONES. HE CAN MAKE THEM LIVE AGAIN.

JEREMIAH 19

YOU HAVE BEEN WEIGHED IN THE BALANCE AND FOUND WANTING.

DANIEL 5:27

GOD'S PEOPLE WILL ONE DAY RETURN FROM EXILE TO THEIR HOMES. YOU CAN TRUST HIM, EVEN WHEN TIMES ARE BAD.

GOD IS SEEING HOW HIS PEOPLE MEASURE UP — ARE THEY TRUE OR CROOKED?

GOD'S PROPHETS OFTEN USE PICTURES TO EXPLAIN HIS MESSAGE.

HOW ELSE DOES GOD SPEAK TO US?

JESUS IS THE RESURRECTION AND THE LIFE

IF JESUS IS THAT, HOW COME WE STILL DIE?

Good point. We think of life as being the bit we're in at the moment, wearing a body. But that's only part of our whole life.

WHAT OTHER LIFE IS THERE?

We are spiritual as well as physical. The spiritual life in us does not need to die when our body dies. It can live for ever.

WHAT, LIKE GHOSTS?

Yes and no! Ghosts are lost and often sad or angry. When we go through death believing in Jesus, we will find a life that is full and happy, filled with joy and peace, and going on for ever in heaven. Jesus has made that possible.

DEAD SITUATIONS IN OUR WORLD AND IN OUR LIFE

OUT OF THE DEPTHS HAVE I CALLED YOU, O LORD:
LORD, HEAR MY VOICE;
IF YOU, LORD, SHOULD NOTE WHAT WE DO WRONG:
WHO THEN, O LORD, COULD STAND?
BUT THERE IS FORGIVENESS WITH YOU:
SO THAT YOU SHALL BE REVERED.
I WAIT FOR THE LORD, MY SOUL WAITS FOR HIM:
AND IN HIS WORD IS MY HOPE.

(–FROM PSALM 130–)   —AMEN—

Holy Week

Passion (Palm) Sunday

Thought for the day

Jesus rides into Jerusalem cheered by the crowds. Days later, crowds will be clamoring for his death.

Readings

Liturgy of the Palms:
Matthew 21:1–11

Liturgy of the Passion:
Isaiah 50:4–7
Philippians 2:6–11
Matthew 26:14—27:66

Aim: To look at Jesus as both hero and failure in the world's eyes.

Starter

Join in the Palm Sunday procession if there is one. Otherwise, join in a procession with the younger children, with branches and possibly even a donkey.

Teaching

Begin by reading the passage from Matthew 21. Look at a palm cross and unwind it so they can see it as a palm leaf, which reminds us of how the people reacted when Jesus rode into Jerusalem on a donkey. Why were they giving him this hero's welcome? Make a note of their ideas on a sheet of paper; these may include such things as:

- They loved Jesus because he had been making people well.
- Jesus looked as if he really was the Messiah they were waiting for.
- They wanted a leader who would help them throw the Romans out.
- Jesus made them think about life in a more exciting way.

Now look at the passage from Philippians 2. Fold the palm leaf into the shape of a cross. What are our palm crosses reminding us now? The people were expecting Jesus to be powerful in the world's way, but instead he was a Servant King, and the kingdom is in people's hearts, not in a particular country. The triumphant procession into Jerusalem was going to lead Jesus straight on towards the cross—no longer a hero, but a complete failure. And yet it was his complete obedience even in this suffering and failure, with most people refusing to under-

stand his mission, which actually turned it all into a fantastic victory, setting us free in a way nothing else could.

Praying

Give thanks to the Lord, for he is good;
his love endures forever.
In my anguish I cried to the Lord,
and he answered by setting me free.
The Lord is with me; I will not be afraid.
Give thanks to the Lord, for he is good;
his love endures forever. Amen.

(From Psalm 118)

Activities

The activity sheet encourages them to look at the way Jesus turns accepted values of power and patterns of kingship upside down. They will also be looking at crowd behavior, and how Jesus tried to teach them through the nature of his entry into Jerusalem, addressing some of their real and false hopes and expectations.

Discussion starters

1. What particular details did you notice in this reading of the crucifixion?

2. Why did Jesus choose not to call on all the angels to be at his disposal? (Matthew 26:53–54)

Notes

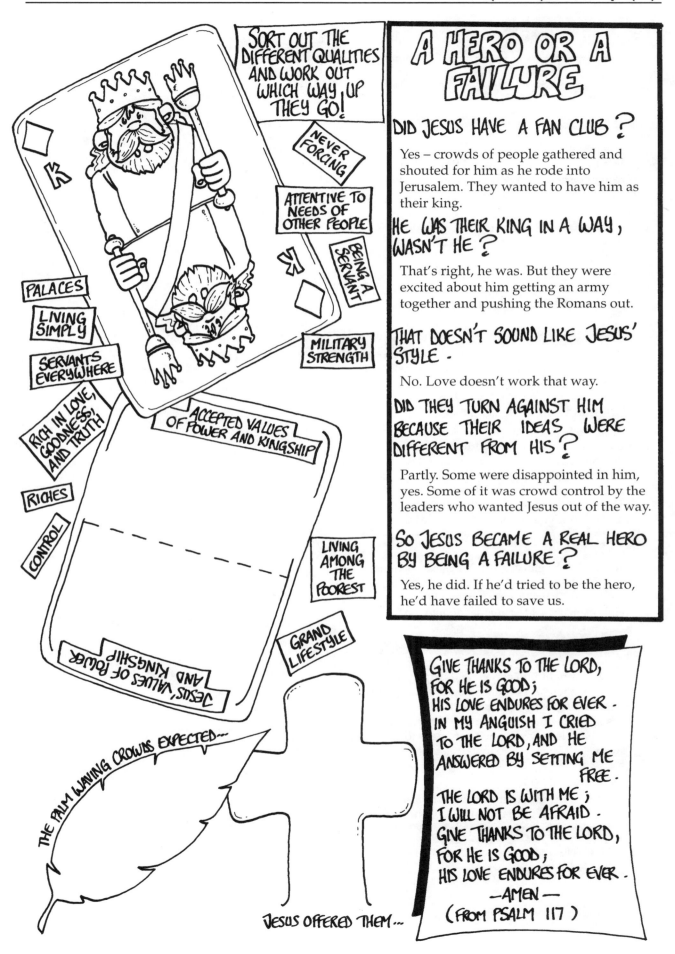

SORT OUT THE DIFFERENT QUALITIES AND WORK OUT WHICH WAY UP THEY GO!

NEVER FORCING

ATTENTIVE TO NEEDS OF OTHER PEOPLE

BEING A SERVANT

PALACES

LIVING SIMPLY

SERVANTS EVERYWHERE

RICH IN LOVE, GOODNESS, AND TRUTH

MILITARY STRENGTH

RICHES

CONTROL

ACCEPTED VALUES OF POWER AND KINGSHIP

LIVING AMONG THE POOREST

GRAND LIFESTYLE

JESUS' VALUES OF POWER AND KINGSHIP

THE PALM WAVING CROWDS EXPECTED...

JESUS OFFERED THEM...

A HERO OR A FAILURE

DID JESUS HAVE A FAN CLUB?

Yes – crowds of people gathered and shouted for him as he rode into Jerusalem. They wanted to have him as their king.

HE WAS THEIR KING IN A WAY, WASN'T HE?

That's right, he was. But they were excited about him getting an army together and pushing the Romans out.

THAT DOESN'T SOUND LIKE JESUS' STYLE -

No. Love doesn't work that way.

DID THEY TURN AGAINST HIM BECAUSE THEIR IDEAS WERE DIFFERENT FROM HIS?

Partly. Some were disappointed in him, yes. Some of it was crowd control by the leaders who wanted Jesus out of the way.

SO JESUS BECAME A REAL HERO BY BEING A FAILURE?

Yes, he did. If he'd tried to be the hero, he'd have failed to save us.

GIVE THANKS TO THE LORD, FOR HE IS GOOD; HIS LOVE ENDURES FOR EVER. IN MY ANGUISH I CRIED TO THE LORD, AND HE ANSWERED BY SETTING ME FREE. THE LORD IS WITH ME; I WILL NOT BE AFRAID. GIVE THANKS TO THE LORD, FOR HE IS GOOD; HIS LOVE ENDURES FOR EVER.
— AMEN —
(FROM PSALM 117)

Easter

Easter Day

Thought for the day

It is true. Jesus is alive for all time. The Lord of life cannot be held by death. God's victory over sin and death means that new life for us is a reality.

Readings

Acts 10:34, 37–43
Colossians 3:1–4
John 20:1–9

Aim: To celebrate the good news of Easter.

Starter

A time of praise, with everyone playing instruments or singing and dancing to recorded music suitable for this age group.

Teaching

Read both the John and the Matthew account of the Resurrection noticing the similarities and the differences, and looking for the central truth in both accounts. Talk about how the different characters might have felt, and why they behaved as they did. Then read the section of Peter's speech in Acts and link this with the accounts they have just read.

Praying

To God be the glory! great things he has done;
so loved he the world that he gave us his Son;
who yielded his life, an atonement for sin,
and opened the life-gate that all may go in.

Activities

Paint posters to express the meaning of Easter. These can be brought into church and displayed there, or used on the church notice boards. The group can work individually or in pairs and threes. The sheet has space for them to plan and design their work, and there is a wordsearch for them to make and swap.

Discussion starters

1. Look at the different reactions of those who were at the tomb. What convinced them that the Resurrection was a real event?

2. How is Jesus' resurrection life different from before he died?

To GOD BE THE GLORY!
GREAT THINGS HE HAS DONE;
SO LOVED HE THE WORLD
THAT HE GAVE US HIS SON;
WHO YIELDED HIS LIFE,
AN ATONEMENT* FOR SIN,
AND OPENED THE LIFE-GATE
THAT ALL MAY GO IN.

* ATONEMENT = PAYING THE PENALTY, MAKING AMENDS

NOT DEAD, BUT ALIVE!

WAS JESUS COMPLETELY DEAD ON GOOD FRIDAY?

Yes. The Romans needed to make quite sure of that. They pierced his side with a sword, too. He was well and truly dead.

HOW DID HE COME TO LIFE?

Nobody watched it happen, so we don't know. But plenty of people saw him alive afterwards, and the tomb empty.

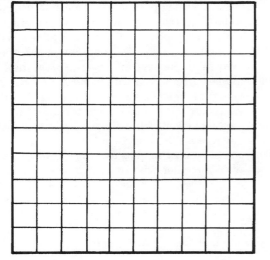

PLAN AND DESIGN YOUR POSTER — TRY TO EXPRESS WHAT EASTER REALLY MEANS. IN ANY WAY YOU LIKE!

RESURRECTION WORDSEARCH

WORDS TO FIND →

Second Sunday of Easter

Thought for the day

Through the risen Jesus we have a living hope which will never spoil or fade.

Readings

Acts 2:42–47
1 Peter 1:3–9
John 20:19–31

Aim: To explore the way different people come to faith.

Starter

*I know what this is, it's a…*Pass around the group an ordinary object such as a sieve. Each person mimes a different way of using it. (For instance, someone might use it as a tennis racket, someone else as a hat, and someone else as a ladle. The uses can be as ridiculous as they like.)

Teaching

We are all different, and we all have different ways of doing things, as we have just seen! Today we are going to look at the different ways people were convinced that Jesus was alive again, and the different ways people find they come to faith today; there isn't just one way that is valid.

Have a sheet with the heading, "Why I believe Jesus is alive," and find the resurrection accounts so that people can refer to them. Go through some of the characters we were looking at last week, and as you mention them work together as a group to put into their words what seems to have clinched it for them (for example, Mary: "I met him in the garden and he talked to me by name.") Look at Mary Magdalene, the other women, the guards, Peter and John in this way.

Now write up Thomas' name, and read together today's gospel. Why might Thomas not have been with the others on the first occasion? (We don't know, but it helps to imagine around the story.) Why might he have made sure he was there exactly a week later? What might he have been hoping? What might he have been dreading? What finally convinced Thomas? (Write this up with the others.)

Now look at all the reasons on the chart. Are there any reasons that are possible for us? (Believing what someone we trust has told us; meeting Jesus when we're together with other believers; meeting Jesus on our own when we are upset or in great need.) Point out that overwhelmingly it seems to be contact with the living person of Jesus that really convinces people, rather than argument and physical proof, though these certainly help to prepare us for believing. Add to the chart other reasons they have met (or known in their own experience) for people coming to a real faith (such as learning about Jesus at church, seeing Christian behavior in their family and their upbringing, seeing the effects of unchristian behavior in society).

Look again at the way Jesus recognizes where Thomas is, and talks to him through it. That's what Jesus will always do. If we genuinely want to know the truth, he will help us to see it, starting from where we are and using our past experiences, both good and bad, in bringing us to faith along a path we can understand and manage to follow.

Praying

My Lord and my God!
My Lord and my God!

Activities

The activity sheet helps to reinforce the teaching and the discussion about ways to faith, including our own, and there is a maze game to make. They will each need some card and a marble for this.

Discussion starters

1. How do you think you might have felt if you had been there that evening when Jesus appeared in the room? Does Jesus appear among us today?

2. Is there any way we can be sure that someone is speaking with God-given authority, rather than personal aggrandizement?

Notes

"WHY I BELIEVE JESUS IS ALIVE"

MARY MAGDALENE

A ROMAN SOLDIER GUARDING THE TOMB

PETER AND JOHN

THOMAS

MY LORD AND MY GOD! MY... LORD... AND... MY... GOD!

YOU!

COMING TO FAITH

WHAT DOES IT MEAN TO COME TO FAITH?

It means to come to know that God is real, that he loves us, and that, in Jesus, God has saved us from the consequences of evil.

LOTS OF PEOPLE DON'T BELIEVE THAT, DO THEY? WHY DON'T THEY?

Because it seems too good to be true; because they don't see Christians acting any differently from them; because they demand visual proof (which we don't have) and because they have been given a wrong idea of what God is like. Lots of other reasons, too.

I WISH I COULD SHOW PEOPLE IT'S TRUE. GOD HAS MADE ME A NEW PERSON, AND I'D LIKE OTHERS TO KNOW HOW LOVELY HE IS.

You can. Just live that new life he has given you, and love other people to faith. Pray for them, and show them.

SOMETIMES COMING TO FAITH IS A BIT LIKE GOING THROUGH A MAZE.

TIN FOIL DISH

1. CUT STRIPS OF CARD TO MAKE WALLS ALL OVER THE DISH. STICK THEM TO THE SIDES AND BOTTOM WITH STICKY TAPE.

2. MAKE SEVERAL POSSIBLE WAYS TO GET FROM THE START TO THE FINISH.

3. ROLL THE MARBLE FROM ONE END OF THE DISH TO THE OTHER.

START

Third Sunday of Easter

Thought for the day

Jesus explains the Scriptures and is recognized in the breaking of bread.

Readings

Acts 2:14, 22–33
1 Peter 1:17–21
Luke 24:13–35

Aim: To explore the Emmaus story and its relevance to our own journeys.

Starter

Pairs of shoes. Cut out a number of different sized pairs of feet and mix them up. The group has to get them into pairs again, either with everyone being given a foot and trying to find the partner, or with all the feet displayed with letters and numbers around the room, so that the aim is to match number and letter correctly without actually touching any.

Teaching

Today we are looking at a fourteen to sixteen mile walk, which took a lot longer going than coming back.

Read the passage from Luke together, with different people taking the speaking parts. Make a note of *who* is in the story, *where* it happened, *when* it happened and *what* took place. Sometimes it helps us to get down to practical details like this, and we notice things we might otherwise overlook. Suggest it as a useful way for them to think through their reading of the Bible at home. Also look at possible *whys*. Why did Jesus appear to his disciples like this soon after the Resurrection? Was it for his benefit or theirs? What did he want them to understand about his risen life?

Praying

You have shown me the path of life;
your presence will fill me with joy.

Activities

On the activity sheet there is space to record some of their ideas and keep track of the discussion, and they can also match the prophecies about Jesus to the New Testament references, so that they have some idea of the way Jesus was fulfilling what was spoken about him.

Discussion starters

1. What guidelines about evangelization can we learn from the way Jesus helps the two disciples from Emmaus?

2. How can we help newcomers, visitors and ourselves to recognize Jesus in the breaking of bread?

Notes

THE EMMAUS ROAD

WHY DIDN'T THEY RECOGNISE JESUS STRAIGHT AWAY?

Quite often we find people don't immediately recognize the risen Christ. Maybe he looked different. Maybe they were not able to recognize him until they knew who he was.

WHY DIDN'T HE TELL THEM WHO HE WAS?

He was like a teacher, drawing them on by questions to drop into the answer for themselves.

WHY WAS IT THE BREAD-BREAKING THAT CRACKED IT FOR THEM?

They remembered the way Jesus had done that before, and perhaps suddenly understood the last supper.

PUZZLE IT OUT!

WHICH REFERENCES FULFIL THESE PROPHECIES ABOUT THE CHRIST?

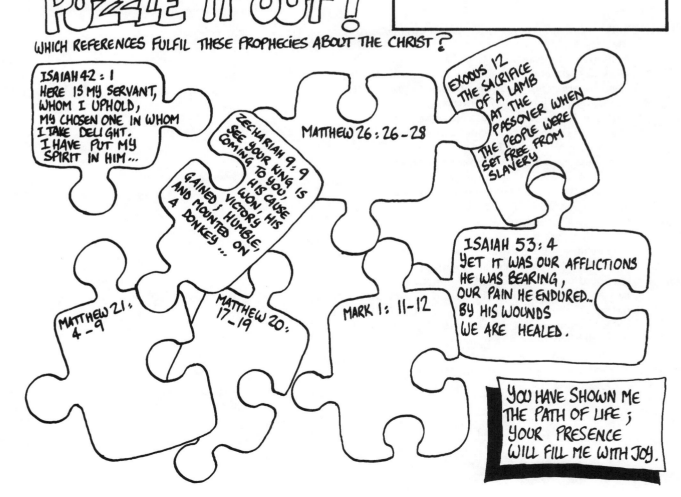

Fourth Sunday of Easter

Thought for the day

Jesus, the Good Shepherd, has come so that we may have life in rich abundance.

Readings

Acts 2:1, 4, 36–41
1 Peter 2:20–25
John 10:1–10

Aim: To look at what God's shepherding involves.

Starter

Animals. First go around the group with each person choosing an animal and doing some appropriate action as they say what they are. Now someone starts by saying and doing their own animal and then naming another from the group. The next person around takes on this identity, copying the original action. They name another animal which the next person around has to take on, and so on. It needs to be played quite fast and is a fairly hilarious game!

Teaching

Today we are going to be thinking about one particular animal: the sheep. There were a lot of sheep around where Jesus lived and that is no doubt why he used them and their shepherds as teaching aids. Read together the gospel for today, stopping after verse 6. Jesus has only been talking about sheep, hasn't he? No wonder they don't understand! What else might he be talking about? Record their ideas.

Now go on to read Jesus' simple words and go over them systematically so that we don't take it for granted: how is Jesus the door for the sheep? Who are the sheep? How do sheep behave if they are always scared? How do they behave when they feel safe? What about *us*—how do people behave when they feel threatened and insecure? How do they behave when they know they are safe, accepted and loved? Help them to see that with Jesus as our shepherd we are set free to live out our lives as our true selves. He provides for us and is there for us, but he won't overpower or try to dominate. When we talk about giving ourselves to God, it doesn't mean that we are giving up our character and personality—only the selfishness and sin which chain and snarl us up so we can't move freely.

Praying

The Lord is my shepherd:
there is nothing I shall want.

Fresh and green are the pastures
where he gives me repose.
Near restful waters he leads me
to revive my drooping spirit.
He guides me along the right path,
he is true to his name.
If I should walk in the valley of darkness,
no evil would I fear.
You are there with your crook and your staff;
with these you give me comfort.

(From Psalm 23)

Activities

On the activity sheet they are encouraged to see what God is and is not, as the Good Shepherd, and there are situations given for them to pray about, where people are in great need of good shepherding.

Provide some card and art materials so that they can make a prayer requests board for the church with a background of sheep on the hillside and the text: "The Lord is my shepherd."

Discussion starters

1. How does the picture of the church community in Acts compare with our own church community? What are the similarities and differences?

2. Do we sometimes treat God as if he were out to destroy or condemn instead of save?

Notes

44

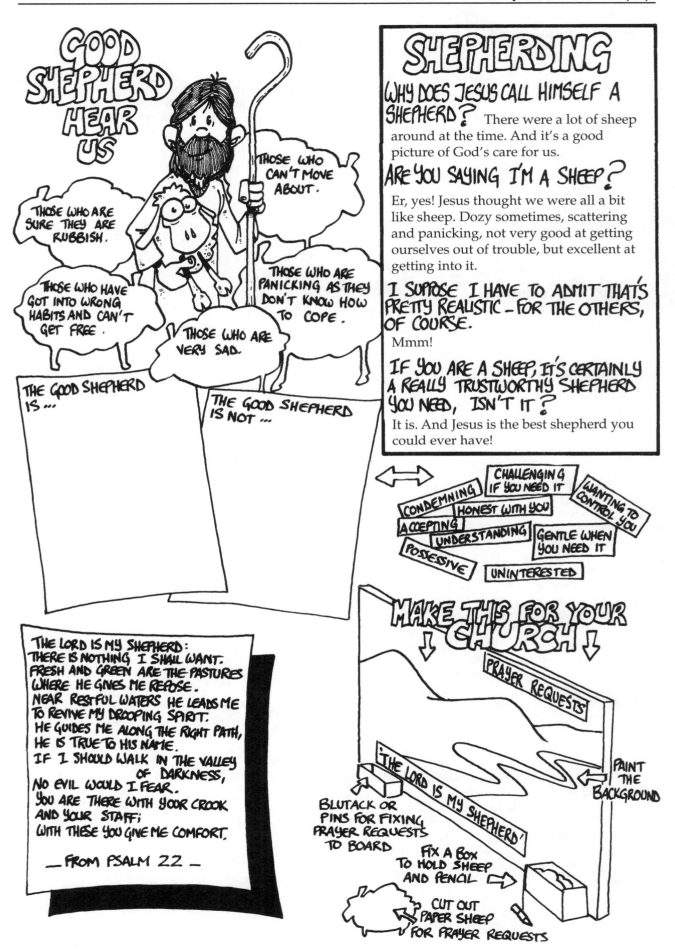

GOOD SHEPHERD HEAR US

- THOSE WHO CAN'T MOVE ABOUT.
- THOSE WHO ARE SURE THEY ARE RUBBISH.
- THOSE WHO HAVE GOT INTO WRONG HABITS AND CAN'T GET FREE.
- THOSE WHO ARE PANICKING AS THEY DON'T KNOW HOW TO COPE.
- THOSE WHO ARE VERY SAD.

THE GOOD SHEPHERD IS ...

THE GOOD SHEPHERD IS NOT ...

SHEPHERDING

WHY DOES JESUS CALL HIMSELF A SHEPHERD? There were a lot of sheep around at the time. And it's a good picture of God's care for us.

ARE YOU SAYING I'M A SHEEP?

Er, yes! Jesus thought we were all a bit like sheep. Dozy sometimes, scattering and panicking, not very good at getting ourselves out of trouble, but excellent at getting into it.

I SUPPOSE I HAVE TO ADMIT THAT'S PRETTY REALISTIC – FOR THE OTHERS, OF COURSE.

Mmm!

IF YOU ARE A SHEEP, IT'S CERTAINLY A REALLY TRUSTWORTHY SHEPHERD YOU NEED, ISN'T IT?

It is. And Jesus is the best shepherd you could ever have!

CHALLENGING IF YOU NEED IT
CONDEMNING
WANTING TO CONTROL YOU
HONEST WITH YOU
ACCEPTING
UNDERSTANDING
GENTLE WHEN YOU NEED IT
POSSESSIVE
UNINTERESTED

MAKE THIS FOR YOUR CHURCH

PRAYER REQUESTS

PAINT THE BACKGROUND

'THE LORD IS MY SHEPHERD'

BLUTACK OR PINS FOR FIXING PRAYER REQUESTS TO BOARD

FIX A BOX TO HOLD SHEEP AND PENCIL

CUT OUT PAPER SHEEP FOR PRAYER REQUESTS

THE LORD IS MY SHEPHERD:
THERE IS NOTHING I SHALL WANT.
FRESH AND GREEN ARE THE PASTURES
WHERE HE GIVES ME REPOSE.
NEAR RESTFUL WATERS HE LEADS ME
TO REVIVE MY DROOPING SPIRIT.
HE GUIDES ME ALONG THE RIGHT PATH,
HE IS TRUE TO HIS NAME.
IF I SHOULD WALK IN THE VALLEY OF DARKNESS,
NO EVIL WOULD I FEAR.
YOU ARE THERE WITH YOUR CROOK
AND YOUR STAFF;
WITH THESE YOU GIVE ME COMFORT.

– FROM PSALM 22 –

Fifth Sunday of Easter

Thought for the day

Jesus is the Way, the Truth and the Life, through whom we can come into the presence of God forever.

Readings

Acts 6:1–7
1 Peter 2:4–9
John 14:1–12

Aim: To see Jesus as the Way, the Truth and the Life, and as the cornerstone on which we are being built up into a spiritual temple.

Starter

Using some road maps, give each couple of people a destination and a place to set out from. They have to work out the best route to take. Share their recommendations.

Teaching

Point out that although they may never have been somewhere, it is still quite easy to get there, providing you know the way. That's why AAA makes all these maps! They recognize that if we didn't know the way, we'd all get hopelessly lost and they'd have to keep coming out to rescue stranded motorists. Today we find Jesus talking to his friends, who are very worried about the future. They know that their leader is in great danger, and they don't really know what is going to happen, or how they are going to be able to cope. It's like lots of us feel at some points in our life. There is confusion, anxiety, and insecurity about the future, and how we will cope.

We are going to find out what Jesus has to offer to anyone in that situation. Read together John 14:1–6. Draw out the lovely reassurance that Jesus gives, and the way he understands how the disciples are feeling, and doesn't tell them to pull themselves together, but gives them a promise that he is going to provide for them personally. Their relationship with him will be like a clear road to walk along which will bring them safely through every danger to heaven.

Now read on to verse 10. Philip (and perhaps the others as well) still doesn't understand that Jesus is the way we are able to see God. We wouldn't be able, as humans, to cope with seeing the full glory of God without it being acted out in a human life—which is why Jesus was born as a human baby.

Look at the living stones passage from 1 Peter, to see how the image here is of Jesus being like a strong cornerstone, or foundation stone, on which

we are all being built, as the Church of God. Again, the picture reminds us of the fact that Jesus is totally reliable, totally faithful, and in him we can find real life, not just the temporary excitements or pleasures that sin offers, but deep, lasting life, in which we are strong and know a security and inner peace which is very satisfying.

Praying

You, Lord, are my rock and my stronghold;
lead me and guide me
for the honor of your name.
Set me free from the net
that has been hidden to catch me;
for you are my refuge.
Into your hand I commit my spirit. Amen.

(From Psalm 31)

Activities

The activity sheet includes a role-play of a road being made, which helps them to explore further what it means for Jesus to be the Way, and also the solid bedrock of our life. There are also examples of other people who have walked the Jesus Way and found it safe and strong.

Discussion starters

1. Why are we sometimes more inclined to go for a code of rules than a personal relationship with the living God?

2. Are there practical ways in which we can give greater witness as a "serving" community?

Notes

46

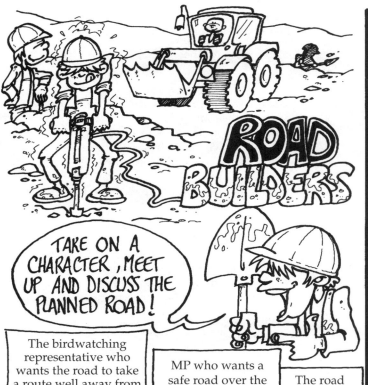

THE WAY, THE TRUTH AND THE LIFE

DOESN'T IT DEPEND ON ME? I CAN LIVE MY WAY, YOU LIVE YOURS.

The trouble with that is when our ways clash. Jesus' way is all about love and respect for God and one another.

BUT THAT'S TOO HARD TO KEEP UP.

True. That's why Jesus said he was the Way – we can do it by living in him.

HOW DO YOU LIVE IN JESUS?

You commit yourself to him, and he gives you his living Spirit, for free.

TAKE ON A CHARACTER, MEET UP AND DISCUSS THE PLANNED ROAD!

The birdwatching representative who wants the road to take a route well away from the nesting birds on the marsh.

MP who wants a safe road over the marshy area, but can offer no more government money.

The road manager who can deal with the marsh and make a strong, safe road, but it will cost more money.

One of the workmen who can explain the layers of stone and reinforced concrete which make it strong and safe. He can recommend this firm's road.

A student whose car got stuck in the marsh on the old track, and who speaks for many who need a good road.

IT TOOK ME YEARS TO TRUST THAT JESUS REALLY IS THE WAY, THE TRUTH AND THE LIFE. NOW MY LIFE FEELS SO MUCH MORE SATISFYING, I WISH I'D TAKEN THE PLUNGE YEARS AGO! IT'S NOT EASIER, MIND YOU, JUST WONDERFUL!

FOLLOWING JESUS THROUGH THE BAD TIMES REALLY HELPED ME GET THROUGH IT!

IF EVER I'M NOT SURE WHICH WAY TO GO, I THINK, 'NOW WHAT WOULD JESUS DO HERE?' AND IT'S ALWAYS THE HONEST, LOVING WAY THAT COMES UP.

I'VE FOLLOWED JESUS ALL MY LIFE AND HE'S NEVER ONCE LET ME DOWN. FRIENDS HAVE, SOMETIMES, BUT JESUS — NEVER!

YOU, LORD, ARE MY ROCK AND MY STRONGHOLD;
LEAD ME AND GUIDE ME FOR THE HONOUR OF YOUR NAME.
SET ME FREE FROM THE NET THAT HAS BEEN HIDDEN TO CATCH ME;
FOR YOU ARE MY REFUGE.
INTO YOUR HAND I COMMIT MY SPIRIT.
(– FROM PSALM 30 –)   — AMEN —

Sixth Sunday of Easter

Thought for the day

The Spirit of truth, given to us, enables us to discern the living, risen Christ.

Readings

Acts 8:5–8, 14–17
1 Peter 3:15–18
John 14:15–21

Aim: To look at the consequences of loving obedience to God.

Starter

Borrow for today either a remote control car or train, or a few computerized games. Try these out together.

Teaching

When you were playing just now, you were in control of the action. Whatever order you gave was obeyed immediately, so you could use the car or hero in the way you needed to. Suppose they'd been able to argue with you, or ignore you or simply refuse to do what you said? You couldn't have used them as effectively. The mission you wanted to accomplish couldn't have happened.

God has plans for his world, and he would love to use us in helping accomplish great things, but he can only do that if we are willing to be under his command, obeying what he says.

Read the gospel for today, and notice how our obedience is not forced, but seen as a sign of our love—if we obey his commands it shows that we really love Jesus; if we don't, it shows we don't really love and trust him at all. We need to look at ourselves and check that out.

Notice, too, what Jesus says will happen once our lives, in tune with our voices, show our love for him. We are promised three things:

1. At Jesus' request, God the Father will give us a helper—the Spirit of Truth—to be with us forever.
2. The Father will love us, as he loves the Son.
3. Jesus will show himself to us, even though in the world's eyes he is invisible.

Now read the passages from 1 Peter 3 and from Acts, looking out for evidence of those three promised things.

Praying

Here I am, Lord—body, heart and soul.
Grant that, with your love,

I may be big enough to reach the world,
and small enough to be at one with you.

(A prayer of Mother Teresa)

Activities

The activity sheet helps them to look at different areas of their life where they can check how far their living is obedient to Jesus' commands, and where it needs changing. There are questions to think about concerning our obedience and our willingness to be used, and some "job advertisements" to apply for, which encourage commitment to Jesus' values.

Discussion starters

1. Do we sometimes expect God to answer our prayers by making us immune from suffering? How does the reading from 1 Peter help us see our relationship with God incorporating suffering?

2. Philip went to a Samaritan town and proclaimed the Christ to them. How can we proclaim the Christ to the people of our time and place?

Notes

USE OF FREE TIME

DEALING WITH ENEMIES

SPENDING

WORK

LOVE GOD LOVE ONE ANOTHER

LOVE LIFE / FRIENDSHIP

OBEDIENCE

DO WE HAVE TO LOOK AT OBEDIENCE? I HATE DOING WHAT I'M TOLD.

So do I. I think most of us do. But yes, obedience is quite important. What about obeying out of love, rather than duty?

LIKE FOLLOWING INSTRUCTIONS FROM A MASTER CHEF TO MAKE MY FAVOURITE MEAL? I'D DO THAT. Yes. Especially if he'd come just to teach you, for free, on his day off.

WOW. I'D DO EVERYTHING HE TOLD ME TO. Well, Jesus gave up everything so you could be freed from sin. It cost him his life, but he didn't charge us anything. It's a free gift.

SO WE OBEY HIM OUT OF LOVE, AND THANKS, THEN? NOT 'COS HE MIGHT PUNISH US.

It's the least we can do.

THIS IS YOUR FOUNDATION TO BUILD ON AND OBEY. HOW DOES YOUR LIFE MEASURE UP?

① LOOK AT YOUR LIFE HONESTLY
② NOTICE ANY AREAS THAT YOU ARE NOT OBEDIENT TO GOD'S LAW OF LOVE.
③ TALK IT OVER WITH GOD, AND AIM TO PUT IT RIGHT WITH HIM.

WOULD YOU BE PREPARED TO LISTEN IF GOD WAS CALLING YOU FOR A PARTICULAR JOB?

HOW DID GOD LAST LET YOU KNOW YOU WERE OUT OF STEP WITH HIM?

(A PRAYER OF MOTHER TERESA)
HERE I AM, LORD — BODY, HEART AND SOUL.
GRANT THAT, WITH YOUR LOVE,
I MAY BE BIG ENOUGH TO REACH THE WORLD,
AND SMALL ENOUGH
TO BE AT ONE WITH YOU.

VACANCIES

WANTED
Young person, lively, friendly – to live out the Christian life in large school and chat the faith informally.

NEEDED
Committed daily prayer support for children and young people trying to rebuild lives after war and terror in Africa.

WANTED
Cheerful giver to give small amounts regularly each week to pay for drop-in center for homeless. Local.

ASSISTANT LEADER
Needed to work with children at vacation club and help them get to know Jesus.

WANTED
Young people who have learned to control their temper to help others through difficult patch. Good listening skills. Understanding and encouragement.

WANTED
Applications welcomed from students taking a year off between school and college – to live and work in city parish. Challenging, but rewarding.

Seventh Sunday of Easter

Thought for the day

God's glory is often revealed in the context of suffering and failure in the world's eyes.

Readings

Acts 1:12–14
1 Peter 4:13–16
John 17:1–11

Aim: To explore the nature of Jesus' glory both on the cross and in heaven.

Starter

Make some rubbings of various coins from different countries. Make a heads and a tails rubbing for each coin.

Teaching

The two sides of a coin both belong equally to the coin, but show us completely different faces of it, and today we are going to look at something which at first sight seems like two different things, but which is actually two sides of the same coin.

First read the account in Acts of the Ascension. Place a large cross cut out of dark colored poster board on the floor, and chalk to record ideas on it, and also a large sun shape with zigzag edges cut out of sunny colored poster board, and crayons to record ideas. Explain that one of the things we are looking at is the cross of Christ, and the other is Christ in glory, having ascended into heaven as a hero. Ask the group to write on the two shapes any words or phrases which come to mind about these two things.

Share what has been suggested in each case, and you will find that they are much more closely linked than you might expect. Read together John 17:1–11, and relate it to your findings recorded on the cross and glory symbols. The Ascension brings us to a place where heaven and earth meet and overlap for a while (overlap the two symbols).

Then read the passage from 1 Peter 4, and listen out for any overlapping of the cross and the glory in that.

Praying

O what a mystery,
meekness and majesty.
Bow down and worship—
this is your God.

(From a song by Graham Kendrick
© Copyright 1986 Kingsway's Thankyou Music/EMI Christian Music Publishing.)

Activities

To express something of this mystery, suggest they create a picture which shows the Ascension from two angles at once—from the earthly and the heavenly viewpoint. They can use symbols and colors, and make the dividing line clear, or mingle the two "plains." On the activity sheet there is space to plan and keep track of ideas, and also some drawings which can be viewed in several different ways.

Discussion starters

1. What do you think the disciples had to learn about Jesus between the Resurrection and the Ascension?

2. Is our society so frightened by suffering, and so bent on avoiding it, that we can no longer appreciate the way it can show us God's glory?

Notes

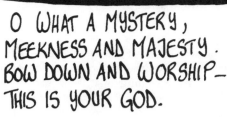

O WHAT A MYSTERY,
MEEKNESS AND MAJESTY.
BOW DOWN AND WORSHIP—
THIS IS YOUR GOD.

(From a song by Graham Kendrick
© Copyright 1986 Kingsway's Thankyou Music/
EMI Christian Music Publishing.)

FROM THE EARTHLY... AND THE HEAVENLY... THE ASCENSION

IDEAS → VIEWPOINT? COLOURS? STYLE?
SYMBOLS? DESIGN?

THE ASCENSION

WHAT'S THAT?

It's Jesus returning to heaven, taking his humanity with him.

DID ANYONE SEE IT HAPPEN?

Yes. The eleven disciples watched him being taken up into heaven.

WHY DID HE LEAVE THEM ON THEIR OWN – I THOUGHT HE'D PROMISED TO BE WITH THEM FOR EVER.

He had – and he wasn't going away in one sense. He was being set free from one physical time zone so he could be right in the center of faithful lives everywhere and everywhen.

2 WAY VIEWING

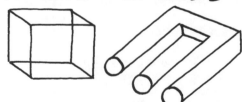

HOW DO YOU THINK THE ASCENSION LOOKED FROM HEAVEN'S POINT OF VIEW? FROM THE DISCIPLES' POINT OF VIEW? OUR POINT OF VIEW?

TRY EXPRESSING JESUS IN GLORY, BOTH GOING AND ARRIVING.

MAKE IT BIG, COLOURFUL, FULL OF MYSTERY AND HOPE!

Pentecost

Thought for the day

With great power the Spirit of God is poured out on the expectant disciples.

Readings

Acts 2:1–11
1 Corinthians 12:3–7, 12–13
John 20:19–23

Aim: To know that the Holy Spirit can also come today.

Starter

If there is a suitable place, start today by building and lighting a small bonfire outdoors. If not, have a metal tray and give everyone a candle each, which they can light and place on the tray. Gather around the fire or the candle flames and watch them for a minute or two in silence.

Teaching

We can't save ourselves, however hard we try, but Jesus did the saving for us. How? (Show a cross.) By dying on the cross, Jesus took all our sin on himself. It was only after his death and Resurrection, and once he had returned to heaven, that the Holy Spirit of God could come pouring out in all its fullness on those who believe in Jesus as their Savior.

Now, sitting around the fire or the candles, read the passage from Acts, imagining this group of Jesus' followers waiting expectantly and obediently.

When they rushed out in their joy and excitement at what God was doing, and saw it all as a great fulfillment of the prophets' longing, it was the first day of the church rushing out to tell others the amazing good news of God's love, powerfully present in his people. It is still going on today. In every generation, people who are expectant and obedient, believing in Jesus as their Savior, can experience that same anointing of the Holy Spirit of almighty God. They don't just know about it, they know it for real, and that is what makes them excited about what God is doing, and what makes them want to rush out and spread the good news.

Praying

Breathe on me, Breath of God,
fill me with life anew,
that I may love what thou dost love
and do what thou wouldst do.
Breathe on me, Breath of God,
till I am wholly thine,
until this earthly part of me
glows with thy fire divine.

Activities

On the activity sheet there is a picture of the Pentecost experience with questions to help them think through the meaning of it, both for the disciples and for themselves. There are also descriptions of other outpourings of the Spirit in the lives of people through the ages since Pentecost.

Discussion starters

1. Think of how we prepare for important exams, interviews or the birth of children. How does this compare with the seriousness we give to seeking the Holy Spirit of God in our lives?

2. We all know there are areas in our church which do not breathe with God's life—yet. What can we do to change that?

Notes

THE WAITING GAME

But do we bother to wait on God?

THEY WERE EXPECTING GOD TO ACT. WHAT ABOUT YOU?

THEY WERE WHERE JESUS HAD TOLD THEM TO BE, AND DOING WHAT HE HAD TOLD THEM TO DO - (WAIT AND PRAY) WHERE ARE YOU?

THEY WANTED THE PRESENCE OF THE REAL GOD MORE THAN ANYTHING ELSE. DO YOU?

THEY MADE THEMSELVES AVAILABLE TO GOD. WHAT ABOUT YOU?

THE HOLY SPIRIT OF GOD

WHAT IS THE HOLY SPIRIT?

The life-giving power of God which strengthens us and makes us holy.

WHY DID THE HOLY SPIRIT COME IN FIRE AND WIND?

Both these had always been symbols of God's presence. And they speak of power and life, light and warmth, direction and movement.

CAN IT COME TO ANYONE?

Yes, to anyone who is open to God and expectant, wanting to receive his life and power.

DOESN'T IT KNOCK YOU OVER?

Sometimes! But the Spirit can also come with great gentleness. God loves you. He knows the best way for you.

AT OUR CHURCH WE ALL PRAYED IN SILENCE. THERE WAS A WONDERFUL SENSE OF GOD'S PEACE. THE HOLY SPIRIT WAS MOVING THERE, IN SUCH GENTLENESS AND LOVE.

LOTS OF US WERE PRAYING TO GOD TO BE PUT RIGHT WITH HIM. SUDDENLY LOTS OF PEOPLE FELL DOWN AND WORSHIPPED GOD AS IF HE WAS REAL! THE HOLY SPIRIT SORTED OUT MANY PEOPLE'S LIVES THAT NIGHT.

BREATHE ON ME, BREATH OF GOD, FILL ME WITH LIFE ANEW, THAT I MAY LOVE WHAT THOU DOST LOVE AND DO WHAT THOU WOULDST DO. BREATHE ON ME, BREATH OF GOD, TILL I AM WHOLLY THINE, UNTIL THIS EARTHLY PART OF ME GLOWS WITH THY FIRE DIVINE.

THERE WERE ONLY 4 OF US PRAYING IN A LITTLE FLAT. BUT AS WE WAITED ON GOD, THE HOLY SPIRIT FLOODED INTO THAT LIVING ROOM AND WE ALL KNEW GOD'S LOVE AND JOY FOR REAL. IT WAS QUITE A SHOCK!

I WAS PRAYING ON MY OWN. I'D HEARD ABOUT THE HOLY SPIRIT AND REALLY WANTED TO MEET GOD AS THE DISCIPLES HAD. SUDDENLY I FELT DELIRIOUSLY HAPPY AND LOVED AND SPECIAL. IT WAS AMAZING! I WANTED TO TELL EVERYONE - IT'S TRUE! GOD'S ALIVE!

IF YOU PRAY THIS - AND MEAN IT - EVERY DAY, GOD WILL BREATHE ON YOU WITH HIS HOLY SPIRIT.

Feasts of the Lord
Trinity Sunday

Thought for the day

The mystery of God—Creator, Redeemer and Sanctifier all at once—is beyond our human understanding, yet closer to us than breathing.

Readings

Exodus 34:4–6, 8–9
2 Corinthians 13:11–13
John 3:16–18

Aim: To look at how we came to see the One God as Trinity.

Starter

Give everyone sketching materials and ask them to draw the same object but from all kinds of different angles and viewpoints.

Teaching

Since today we celebrate the mystery and beauty of the Trinity, we are going to look at how people have come to see God in this way. Point out that the term "Trinity" does not appear anywhere in the Bible, but there are lots of hints and clues in Scripture which have led us to this way of describing God. First of all, what does the word "Trinity" mean?

Show two signs, one saying "Tri" and the other "Unity." Talk together about what each of these means. "Tri" is quite straightforwardly "three": the Father who is Creator, the Son who is Jesus the Redeemer, and the Holy Spirit who is the living Breath of God. "Unity" has the sense of several being united in a kind of team effort, of a group being of one mind, of cooperation and intertwining of ideas and gifts. Put the two sections together so that they overlap and form the word "Trinity," which combines all you have been talking about.

Now fix three small circles of paper on the floor to outline a triangle. In the Trinity the three persons are both distinct and bound up in one being. Sometimes through the history of the Church some Christians have thought of them as so completely distinct (move the circles far apart) that the sense of unity is lost; others have thought of them as so closely bound (move the circles on top of one another) that the sense of community is lost. The truth is that for our great, loving God of mystery and wonder, the "Tri" and the "Unity" are both possible.

Now look through the following references together, looking out for the presence of Creator, Word (Jesus' title) and Spirit, to see how they speak of this mystery which is God, so great that our human minds can't expect to be able to "nail it down."

Genesis 1:1–3
John 1:1–4
Matthew 28:18–20
Romans 8:3–4
Ephesians 3:14–19

Praying

Holy, holy, holy! Lord God almighty!
May the grace of our Lord Jesus Christ
and the love of God
and the fellowship of the Holy Spirit
be with us all evermore. Amen.

Activities

On the activity sheet there is space to link the references to our understanding of God, and they can try to express something of the Trinity nature of God in art forms such as wire sculpture, mobiles or collage.

Discussion starters

1. If the God we worship has been revealed to us as community in unity, and we pray for God's kingdom to come on earth "in the way it happens in heaven," what does that suggest about the way the Church should be operating?
2. Why are we baptized in the name of the Father, Son and Holy Spirit, rather than the one true God?

Notes

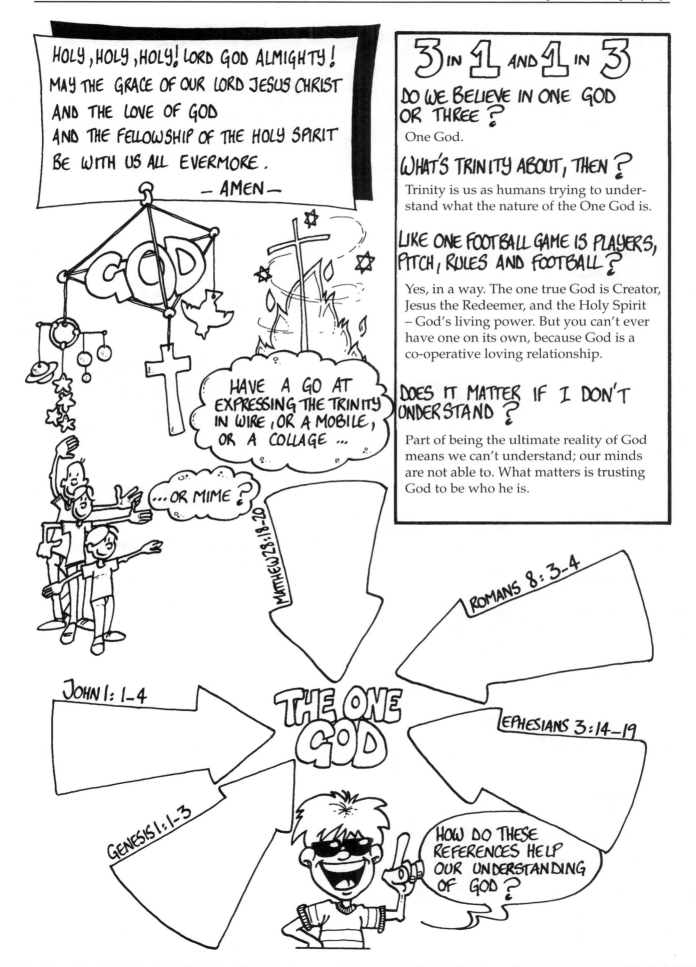

Ordinary Time

Second Sunday in Ordinary Time

Thought for the day
Jesus is recognized and pointed out by John to be God's chosen one.

Readings
Isaiah 49:3, 5–6
1 Corinthians 1:1–3
John 1:29–34

Aim: To explore why the disciples thought Jesus was the Messiah.

Starter
Giant Mastermind. Fix up three chairs as shown below, with three pieces of colored card hung around the back, so only the person behind the chairs can see the colors. In front of the chairs have a length of lining paper marked out as shown. People use crayons or marking pens to record their guess as to the color and position of the hidden colors. The person behind the chairs responds by placing a check for every correct color and for every correct position. Eventually they should be able to work out the exact hidden pattern using reasoning and deduction.

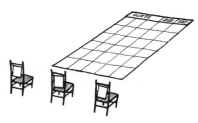

GUESS			Right colour	Right place
●	●	●	✓✓	✓
●	●	●	✓✓✓	✓
		●		

Teaching
Draw their attention to the way we had to work out the answer to that puzzle by going on the information we were given, linked with a "hunch" that our idea was right, and a little help from our friends. That's what the first disciples had to do.

As they read John's gospel, they can look out for the puzzle they were trying to solve (Who's this?), and notice how they did it. Record their observations. What information do we already have about the Messiah? Read the passage from Isaiah, and again record their observations. (One day God's anointed One—the Messiah—would come in person to save them and set them free. It wouldn't be just for the people of Israel but for the whole world.) Who gave them other hints and clues? (John the Baptist; Jesus' conversation.)

Praying
O most merciful Redeemer,
friend and brother,
may I know you more clearly,
love you more dearly,
and follow you more nearly
day by day. Amen.

(The prayer of Richard of Chichester)

Activities
On the activity sheet there is a short sketch in which a group of people talk over their first encounter with Jesus and what impressed them about him. There is also space for them to record their own remembered "first impressions" of Jesus, and how they have changed, or been added to, as they have grown older.

Discussion starters
1. What can we learn about evangelizing from today's gospel?

2. How does John's way of narrating Jesus' Baptism differ from Matthew's? What do both accounts agree about?

Notes

FIRST IMPRESSIONS

CHOOSE SOME FOR EACH PERSON. NOW TAKE A CHARACTER EACH AND HAVE A CONVERSATION ABOUT MEETING JESUS.

- Jesus listens to you.
- He isn't bothered whether you're rich or poor.
- He seems to like you and be interested in you.
- He knows what he's talking about.
- He's happy to put himself out to help you.
- He makes you feel important.
- He's wise, but not at all boastful.
- He enjoys a joke.
- He gives you space.
- He seems to know what you're thinking.

THE CHOSEN ONE OF GOD

WHO SAID THAT?

John the Baptist

HOW DID HE KNOW?

He saw the Spirit come down on him from heaven like a dove.

SO IT WAS SEEING HIM IN PERSON THAT CONVINCED HIM?

Yes.

IS THAT TRUE FOR US AS WELL?

Yes, it is. As you get to know Jesus personally, you find more and more about the living, loving God.

NAME

NAME

NAME

NAME

MY FIRST IMPRESSIONS OF JESUS ...

... AND HOW THEY HAVE CHANGED/ BEEN ADDED TO

O MOST MERCIFUL REDEEMER, FRIEND AND BROTHER, MAY I KNOW YOU MORE CLEARLY, LOVE YOU MORE DEARLY, AND FOLLOW YOU MORE NEARLY DAY BY DAY.
— AMEN —

Third Sunday in Ordinary Time

Thought for the day

The prophecies of Isaiah are fulfilled in a new and lasting way in Jesus of Nazareth.

Readings

Isaiah 8:23—9:3
1 Corinthians 1:10–13, 17
Matthew 4:12–23

Aim: To look at the situation Isaiah was in, and see how prophecy has more than one level.

Starter

Have some small pieces of scratch-board for them to scratch pictures in. These can either be bought, or home-made using colored wax crayons rubbed thickly onto paper and covered with a layer of black wax crayon or waterproof ink.

Teaching

Using an enlarged version of the following map, or an atlas of the Bible, show how Judah was placed, so that they can see why the Assyrians (and later the Babylonians) wanted to conquer it. It would be useful, for trade and communications, to have control of it. Brainstorm and record ideas of how the people may have felt with Assyrian power so close.

Find Jerusalem and explain how Isaiah had been sent to speak out God's words to the people there. He is disturbed by all the social injustice, and lack of honesty and integrity in the way people are living, and can see that a people rejecting God's values of love, justice and mercy is likely to be overtaken by Assyria. Isaiah urges the people to turn back to God and trust him to save them.

Now read today's passage from Isaiah. Remem-bering how the people were feeling, what would they have made of this? Help them to pick up on the sense of hope and reassurance.

Read the passage from Matthew, listening for similarities (place names, language). What is Matthew trying to tell us by the way he quotes the Isaiah reading? (Jesus must be the light and the yoke-breaker we've been waiting for.)

So Isaiah's prophecy meant more than one layer of truth. There is both the immediate hope for a nasty situation and a more universal meaning which can help people of all races, social grouping, financial state and in each age. That is often true of prophecy; it can, like our scratch-pictures, have several different layers, some of which only become clear later on.

Praying

Use this version of the *Nunc Dimittis*—or Simeon's song (Luke 2:29–32):

Lord, now let your servant go in peace:
your word has been fulfilled.
My own eyes have seen the salvation:
which you have prepared in the sight of every people.
A light to reveal you to the nations:
and the glory of your people Israel.

Activities

Using thin card, and the instructions on the activity sheet, make a 3-dimensional model of the word "prophecy." There is also space for thinking about different social injustices in our own world to which Isaiah may well have drawn our attention in the eighth century before Christ.

Discussion starters

1. Find Zebulun and Naphtali on a map. Are there any areas of land (either geographical or spiritual) where we need to invite Jesus to walk?

2. What good news do the people need him to preach there?

Notes

MATTHEW 4 12 - 23 SO GOD'S PROMISE CAME TRUE, JUST AS THE PROPHET ISAIAH HAD SAID.

PROPHECY AND PROPHETS

WHAT IS PROPHECY?

It's the word of God, spoken out to the people by his chosen messengers.

SO THE CHOSEN MESSENGERS ARE PROPHETS?

That's right. Isaiah of Jerusalem was a prophet.

CAN A PROPHECY HAVE A HIDDEN MEANING?

Yes. The people would pick up on what it meant for them in their own situation, but there is often a deeper truth.

COULD PEOPLE ONLY SEE THAT ONCE JESUS HAD COME?

Yes. Jesus filled the prophecies full of new meaning. We say he 'fulfilled' them.

WHAT HAD ISAIAH SAID ABOUT THE AREA ROUND GALILEE?

HOW DID THE PROMISE COME TRUE ???

SIMEON'S SONG (LUKE 2 : 29 -32)

LORD, NOW YOU LET YOUR SERVANT GO IN PEACE : YOUR WORD HAS BEEN FULFILLED.
MY OWN EYES HAVE SEEN THE SALVATION : WHICH YOU HAVE PREPARED IN THE SIGHT OF EVERY PEOPLE.
A LIGHT TO REVEAL YOU TO THE NATIONS : AND THE GLORY OF YOUR PEOPLE ISRAEL.

PROPHECIES ARE OFTEN CHALLENGING

SO HERE IS A CHALLENGE !!!

☆ CAN YOU MAKE A 3D MODEL OF THE WORD PROPHECY USING FOLDED AND CURVED PAPER?

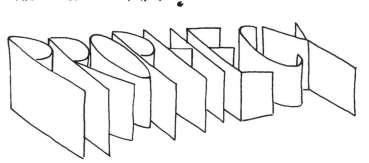

NOTE THE DIFFERENT VIEWING POINTS!

Fourth Sunday in Ordinary Time

1. Is it possible to kid ourselves that we are seeking God when in fact we are self-seeking?

2. In what ways do the poor in spirit become rich?

Thought for the day

Happy are the poor in spirit, who are aware of their need of God.

Readings

Zephaniah 2:3; 3:12–13
1 Corinthians 1:26–31
Matthew 5:1–12

Aim: To look at the Beatitudes and their meaning.

Starter

Have an travel map (any area) and give out map references which they have to find to discover the route from one place to another.

Teaching

Read the passage from Zephaniah, noticing that it is the humble, seeking God, who will be saved in the end, rather than the self-seeking and powerful. The passage from Corinthians reinforces this, recognizing that the followers of Christ are often the weak and unremarkable, except that in Christ they end up doing remarkable things.

Now look at Jesus' teaching in today's gospel, using a version which is accessible to them. Draw out the importance of recognizing our need of God, of hungering and thirsting for him, and wanting to put God first in our lives. It all turns selfishness and self-seeking on its head, and sets us on a giving rather than a getting way of life.

Praying

Lord our God,
help us to love you with all our hearts,
to seek after you and find you,
to long for what you long for
and rejoice at what gives you joy.

Activities

On the activity sheet the Beatitudes are looked at in terms of their implications for us and our life choices. They can also get the sense of re-aligning our lives to God by placing a magnet under the paper where it says "God's way" and placing a paper clip fixed to "My life" on top of the paper so that it settles firmly on the magnet.

Notes

MY LIFE

① CUT THIS OUT AND FIX A PAPER CLIP HERE.

② TAPE A MAGNET UNDER THE PAPER, UNDER THE 'GOD'S WAY' SIGN.

③ PLACE THE 'MY LIFE' SIGN WITH ITS PAPER CLIP OVER THE 'GOD'S WAY' SIGN.

④ WATCH HOW IT LINES UP. ADJUST THE PAPER CLIP UNTIL YOUR LIFE SETTLES NATURALLY IN LINE WITH 'GOD'S WAY'.

GOD'S WAY

THE BEATITUDES

WHAT DOES THAT MEAN?

Jesus taught the people how to live God's way. Part of this teaching is telling them what makes a person happy and blessed.

WHO DOES JESUS RECKON IS HAPPY AND BLESSED?

Not the ones you'd expect – not the rich and famous or clever.

WHO THEN?

Those who realize their need of God, those who hunger and thirst for what's right, those who are pure in their thinking.

WHAT IF THEY GET TEASED?

Jesus says we're specially blessed if we're treated badly because we're doing good. And we'll be rewarded in heaven.

WHO ARE THE 'BLESSED'?

① _____ ② _____
③ _____ ④ _____
⑤ _____ ⑥ _____
⑦ _____ ⑧ _____
    ⑨ _____

HOW WOULD OUR LIVES HAVE TO CHANGE?

LORD OUR GOD,
HELP US TO LOVE YOU WITH ALL OUR HEARTS,
TO SEEK AFTER YOU AND FIND YOU,
TO LONG FOR WHAT YOU LONG FOR
AND REJOICE AT WHAT GIVES YOU JOY.

ARE THE BEATITUDES REALISTIC? HOW DO THEY CHANGE LIVES?

Fifth Sunday in Ordinary Time

Thought for the day

We are commissioned to live so that we shine like lights which direct others to God, the source of Light.

Readings

Isaiah 58:7–10
1 Corinthians 2:1–5
Matthew 5:13–16

Aim: To look at the way Christians are called to be salt and light, and the practical implications of this.

Starter

Bring along some mirrors and flashlights and in small groups experiment to get the light shining all over the place by using the mirrors. Help them to see that this is only possible when the mirrors are turned to reflect the light.

Teaching

When you have lots of reflectors they will pass on the light outwards, and anyone wanting to find out more about where the real light is has only to line themselves up with a mirror and look in that direction. It's the same with us as Christians—if we are shining with Christ's light, then other people will notice, and if they want to find where we are getting our light from, they only have to face the direction our lives are facing.

Read together the gospel passage for today, listening out for this teaching.

What else did Jesus say we were to be like? Salt. In this instance, Jesus talks about the seasoning quality of salt; just a tiny amount is enough to make all the difference to a dish by bringing out the best flavor in the other ingredients. And that means that we as Christians are to be the kind of people who bring the best out in others, enabling them to feel valued and respected. Salt and light are very practical things. The problem is that the people are not being salt and light in their world. They may be good at talking about godly living but they aren't actually living it out. God wants to see some action, both in their lives and ours.

On a sheet have the headings taken from Isaiah (free the oppressed, share food with the hungry, etc.) and collect suggestions for ways we are and ways we could be doing these things in our world, as individuals, as a church community and in society.

Praying

Lord God,
let us not just hear and talk about
being salt and light;
help us to *be* salt and light
so that we make a difference. Amen.

Activities

On the activity sheet there is space to record some ideas for action, following today's teaching, and there is the outline for a role-play to bring out the way we all prefer to talk about things rather than actually getting our hands dirty.

Discussion starters

1. What do the qualities and usefulness of salt tell us about our calling as Christians?

2. How can we be effective light in the world?

Notes

LORD GOD,
LET US NOT JUST HEAR AND TALK ABOUT
BEING SALT AND LIGHT;
HELP US TO BE SALT AND LIGHT
SO THAT WE MAKE A DIFFERENCE.
— AMEN —

SALT AND LIGHT

BEING SALT SOUNDS A BIT LIKE BEING A SERVANT, TO ME.

That's right – it's putting other people first, and helping without making a great show of it.

DOES THAT MEAN YOU CAN'T BE A CHRISTIAN AND BE SELF-ASSERTIVE?

No, but it does mean we can't be pushy and on a power trip all the time.

WHAT ABOUT BEING LIGHT?

God's light shines in us whenever we're honest, faithful, good and caring Christians.

WHAT DO WE DO WHEN THEY NOTICE?

Point them towards God, who makes you shine.

WHAT CAN WE DO ABOUT IT?

THE HOMELESS

THOSE IMPRISONED BY POVERTY

THE HUNGRY

YOU GO TO CHURCH AND PRAY EACH DAY. YOU THINK THE CHARITY SHOULD PRAY ABOUT THE PEOPLE INSTEAD OF ASKING FOR MONEY.

YOU ARE GLAD TO SEE THE YOUNG PEOPLE DOING SOMETHING USEFUL FOR ONCE BUT, NO, YOU CAN'T HELP AS WHISKY HAS JUST GONE UP IN PRICE.

YOU ARE SINGING AND COLLECTING WITH YOUR YOUTH GROUP FOR CHARITY

YOU DON'T THINK PEOPLE SHOULD BE POOR, BUT YOU CAN'T AFFORD TO HELP AS YOU'VE JUST BOUGHT A NEW VOLVO

YOU THINK THE PROBLEM OF POVERTY IS SO BIG THAT THIS LITTLE EFFORT ISN'T WORTH DOING

Sixth Sunday in Ordinary Time

Thought for the day
To live God's way is to choose the way of life.

Readings
Sirach 15:15–20
1 Corinthians 2:6–10
Matthew 5:17–37

Aim: To see how Jesus fulfills the Law.

Starter
Getting the whole picture. Cut up a large poster or picture into nine squares, and number the backs of the pieces. Arrange them upside down, but in the right order. Work out a quiz based on the ideas below but adapted to suit your group. Each time a question is answered correctly a piece of the picture is turned over, until eventually the whole picture is revealed.

Ideas for quiz questions:

What's their latest release?

What are their names?

How old are they?

Name two of their hits.

What are the lyrics of……?

Who sings?

Who plays……?

What does……like to eat?

Where do they come from?

Teaching
Gradually, as we had more information, we got the whole picture. It was rather like that for the Jewish people, because they had gradually understood more and more about who God was and what he was like. When Jesus came and lived among them, he built on all that knowledge and experience, and showed them the whole picture by his life, death and resurrection.

Read the Matthew passage to see where the people were coming from, and compare Jesus' teaching with the commandments concerned. How was it the same and how did it take the law and fill it with more complete meaning? There is space on the activity sheet to record ideas, or you may prefer to use a flipchart or large sheet of paper and copy the activity sheet format on to this.

Praying
Savior, breathe forgiveness o'er us,
all our weakness thou dost know.
Thou didst tread this earth before us,
thou didst feel its keenest woe.
Lone and dreary, faint and weary,
through the desert thou didst go.

Spirit of our God, descending,
fill our hearts with heavenly joy.
Love with every passion blending,
pleasure that can never cloy.
Thus provided, pardoned, guided,
nothing can our peace destroy.

Activities
On the activity sheet there are some examples of Celtic knotwork to copy using string, craft glue and colored paper or card. There is also space to explore the ideas arising from Jesus' teaching, suggesting that a "murderous" or destructive attitude can be just as deadly as actual murder.

Discussion starters
1. How do rules help, and in what sense are guidelines sometimes more useful?

2. Why is it that when we have chosen to face life we still want to behave as if we are facing the other way?

Notes

USE STRING AND GLUE ON COLOURED PAPER!

CELTIC KNOTWORK!

A MATTER OF LIFE AND DEATH

WHAT IS?

The way we live.

YOU MEAN ALL THE EXCITING STUFF IS OUT?

The really exciting stuff is in! But I know sin looks tempting because it looks (and feels) nice. At first. But not in the long run, and not for other people.

I SUPPOSE WE NEED TO KEEP THAT IN MIND WHEN WE'RE TEMPTED?

Yes, and God's power helps us stay strong. God's way of love is the way to life.

HOW LONG FOR?

Ever.

MURDER

[A DESTRUCTIVE ATTITUDE!]

SAVIOUR BREATHE FORGIVENESS O'ER US,
ALL OUR WEAKNESS THOU DOST KNOW.
THOU DIDST TREAD THIS EARTH BEFORE US,
THOU DIDST FEEL ITS KEENEST WOE.
LONE AND DREARY, FAINT AND WEARY,
THROUGH THE DESERT THOU DIDST GO.
SPIRIT OF OUR GOD DESCENDING,
FILL OUR HEARTS WITH HEAVENLY JOY.
LOVE WITH EVERY PASSION BLENDING,
PLEASURE THAT CAN NEVER CLOY.
THUS PROVIDED, PARDONED, GUIDED,
NOTHING CAN OUR PEACE DESTROY.

LIKE WHAT, FOR INSTANCE...

Seventh Sunday in Ordinary Time

Thought for the day

We are called to be holy; to be perfect in our generous loving, because that is what God our Father is like.

Readings

Leviticus 19:1–2, 17–18
1 Corinthians 3:16–23
Matthew 5:38–48

Aim: To explore the implications of our call to holiness.

Starter

Friend or foe? Have a number of qualities written on cards which can be sorted into the "friend" or "foe" pile. Ideas for the cards:

- Lets you down all the time
- Lends you their pen when you have forgotten yours
- Mistreats someone you love
- Accuses you so you get the blame unjustly
- Puts you down in front of other people
- You can trust them to keep a secret
- Makes you pay for everything and never offers to help
- Cheers you up when you're feeling down
- Winds you up constantly
- Waits for you if you're late out
- Keeps your place in the line
- Understands when you don't agree about something

Teaching

Read together Matthew 5:38–48. Begin by clearing up a common misunderstanding about Christians and enemies. There are always some people we get along well with, and others we dislike. It is natural to feel hostile to anyone who treats you or your loved ones badly. God knows about all this. He knows we have both friends and enemies, and he doesn't want us to pretend about our true feelings—it's much healthier to take them out and look at them so that we are aware of what's going on inside us. Jesus is teaching us how to deal with our enemies, and our feelings.

We are not told to *like* our enemies, but to treat them with love. That means being absolutely fair and honest with them, however dishonest they are with us. It means treating them with respect and consideration, however much they insult and scorn us. That way we will be showing them the kind of behavior we consider right, and we won't be dragged down into behaving as badly as they are.

What Jesus doesn't mean is for us to lie down like doormats for people to walk over! If an enemy is bullying us, for instance, the loving way to treat them is not to suffer it all in an agony of silence and fear, but to tell them that they are behaving badly, and let someone in authority know, so that the situation can be properly dealt with. That is kinder to them than letting them carry on bullying without being confronted.

We also need to look at our own behavior. Are we sometimes behaving as enemies to people in our own families, for instance? Are there people we despise, or treat badly, or refuse to help?

Being holy means behaving in a godly way to everyone, without taking some for granted, or drawing a line around a particular group we give ourselves permission to hate.

Praying

Give me understanding, Lord,
that I may keep your law of love
with my whole life and energy and will.
I pray now for those I dislike
and find it hard to get along with.
Teach me how to treat them with love. Amen.

Activities

On the activity sheet there is a form for them to fill in which will actually benefit someone else. And there are instructions for playing a competitive game (such as the game of *Life,* or snakes and ladders) with someone else's gain as our priority for a change.

Discussion starters

1. Is Jesus' teaching unworkable? Or is it simply more challenging than we would like to take on seriously?

2. How does our society's concern with self-value and self-assertion fit in with our Christian faith, and where does it clash?

Notes

THIS IS TO CERTIFY THAT _____
IS PROMISED A
* CAR WASH
* WASHING UP SESSION
* BABY SITTING SESSION
(* DELETE AS APPROPRIATE.)

COMPLETELY FREE of CHARGE

DONATED IN LOVE BY _____
DATE _____

LOVE YOUR ENEMIES

HOW CAN YOU DO THAT?

You don't have to like them. But you can pray for them and treat them with consideration and generosity.

WHAT, EVEN IF THEY MAKE YOUR LIFE HELL?

Yes.

THAT'S CRAZY!

True. It's the same kind of crazy, generous love that God has for all of us.

IF YOU ARE IN FRONT, SWAP WITH SOMEONE BEHIND YOU.	USE THE NEXT LADDER TO GO DOWN	ADD YOUR SCORE TO THE NEXT PLAYER'S SO THEY CAN USE IT.
IF YOUR SCORE IS HIGHER THAN THE NEXT PLAYER'S, SWAP SCORES.	MISS A GO VOLUNTARILY AND LET THE NEXT PLAYER TAKE IT AS THEIRS.	LET THE NEAREST PLAYER GO UP THE SNAKE YOU WENT DOWN.

⇧ CUT THESE OUT AND PLACE FACE DOWN IN A PILE. ⇧

USE A SNAKES AND LADDERS GAME. THE GAME IS WON WHEN ALL PLAYERS GET TO THE END. WHENEVER YOU THROW A 6, YOU TAKE A CARD AND DO WHAT IT SAYS.

LOOK WHAT AMAZING THINGS CAN HAPPEN WHEN PEOPLE DO MANAGE TO TREAT THEIR ENEMIES WITH LOVE!

THE TIMES

SOUTH AFRICA
MANDELA URGES THE PEOPLE TO FORGIVE AND WORK TOGETHER NOW!

GIVE ME UNDERSTANDING, LORD,
THAT I MAY KEEP YOUR LAW
OF LOVE WITH MY WHOLE LIFE
AND ENERGY AND WILL.
I PRAY NOW
FOR THOSE I DISLIKE AND
FIND IT HARD TO GET ON WITH.
TEACH ME
HOW TO TREAT THEM
WITH LOVE.
—AMEN—

TURN THE WORLD'S RULES UPSIDE DOWN!

AM I BEHAVING LIKE AN ENEMY TO ANYONE?

Eighth Sunday in Ordinary Time

Thought for the day

God is creative and good; seeking his rule, as our priority, will mean that everything else falls into place.

Readings

Isaiah 49:14–15
1 Corinthians 4:1–5
Matthew 6:24–34

Aim: To look at priorities in life in the light of Jesus' teaching.

Starter

First things first. Give each person in the group a piece of card to hold, on which is written a possible priority. Holding their cards, they arrange themselves in order of priority according to the situation you give them. Priorities might include:

- Buying food before the shop closes
- Finishing the crossword puzzle
- Going to bed early
- Washing your hair
- Praying
- Doing your homework
- Getting to work on time
- Reading the Bible

Teaching

First read the passage from Matthew 6. What is the priority that Jesus suggests is best? Jesus is reassuring his listeners that they really can trust God completely. What kind of God is he? What is he like?

Look now at the creation narrative in Genesis, searching in it for hints and clues about God's nature, and write down all the ideas. These can be placed around the outside of the creation picture on the sheet.

Praying

Oh give thanks to the Lord,
for he is good,
for his steadfast love endures for ever. Amen.

(From Psalm 136)

Activities

There are places on the activity sheet for them to discuss and name some of the usual worries they have.

Take some of these out and look at them, working out together which ones are not worth wasting our energies on, and which need to be properly addressed. They can pray together and for one another, about some of the worries raised.

Discussion starters

1. How is God's creative nature still apparent today?

2. What is the difference between loving concern for people and the kind of anxious living Jesus recommends we reject?

Notes

1ST THINGS 1ST

WHAT DOES COME FIRST?

Often it's ourselves, our wants and our worries.

IS THERE A BETTER WAY?

Yes. Jesus advises us to go after God first – as a priority.

WHAT ABOUT ALL THE WORRIES?

He says that once we get our priorities right we won't find everything makes us worry anymore.

DOES GOD GIVE YOU AN EASY LIFE THEN?

No. But he provides you with all you need to cope.

NAME THE WORRY	NOT WORTH THE ENERGY	NEEDS TO BE ADDRESSED. HOW?

OH GIVE THANKS TO THE LORD,
FOR HE IS GOOD,
FOR HIS STEADFAST LOVE
ENDURES FOR EVER.
—AMEN—
(FROM PSALM 135)

Ninth Sunday in Ordinary Time

Thought for the day

Wise listeners build their lives up on the strong rock of the word of God.

Readings

Deuteronomy 11:18, 26–28, 32
Romans 3:21–25, 28
Matthew 7:21–27

Aim: To explore what it means to build our lives on the rock of God's teaching.

Starter

Beforehand make a simple picture of a house, cut from colored paper. At the same time cut enough identical pieces for each couple of people in the group to make up the same picture. (You might have background pieces of green and blue, a different green hill, the main house shape, different colored window and door shapes.) The pieces will need to be put together in the right order and position if they are to look exactly like the original.

First show the original to everyone for twenty or thirty seconds, and then cover it up while they all make their own pictures. Then show the original again to check who got it exactly right.

Teaching

They probably noticed in that activity that they had to concentrate carefully during the viewing time so as to pick up and store as much vital information as possible. Then, building on that, they were able to get close to the right picture. Today we are looking at something Jesus said to some of those who came to listen to him. They claimed to be his followers but in fact their lives showed no attempt to carry out God's teaching. Jesus always hated any kind of hypocrisy—or saying one thing and doing another. Being full of truth and integrity himself, he was disturbed by people thinking God could be fooled by what they might say. God matches up what we say with what we do, and he can easily tell if we are pretending.

Read Matthew 7:21–27. If we really listen to what Jesus tells us—listen with our heart and will as well as our ears—we shall be wanting to use what we have heard in the building of our lives. If, on the other hand, we assume those words are not really meant for us, and have no intention of acting on them, we shall be throwing away all that Jesus offers, and end up building our lives on things that give way on us and let us down, instead of the solid rock which we can always rely on.

But there is a problem. Being human we can genuinely want to build on the right foundations, and mean it at the time we say that we believe in God and want to be his followers. Then often we find ourselves getting carried away living in the same old bad habits, and pleasing ourselves yet again. In the Old Testament the people had found the same problem. They had tried all kinds of ways to remind themselves of God's Law so that they would remember how to live his way. Read the Deuteronomy 11 passage to see how seriously they tried.

To some extent it worked, but then the reminders themselves would start to become more important to people than what they were there for! With the coming of Jesus, and the filling of our lives with the Holy Spirit of God, there was a drastic and exciting change to this state of affairs. Paul talks about it in today's passage from Romans: we know we can't manage it on our own, but through God's freely given grace, won for us by Jesus, the impossible becomes possible. Read Romans 3:21–25, 28.

Not only can we listen to Jesus' words, and make the decision to build on that strong foundation, but God will also be there with us in the work of building.

Praying

O God, the strength of all who put their trust in you,
we know that, being human,
we can do no good thing without you.
We ask you to give us your gift of grace
so that we can live lives that are pleasing to you.
Amen.

Activities

On the activity sheet there is a building plan to fill in, to help them put into practice God's teaching in their everyday lives. These can be decorated, cut out and placed in envelopes to be offered and blessed in church, before being given back after the service so they can be used in daily living.

Discussion starters

1. What does it mean to "do the will of my Father," rather than saying only, "Lord, Lord!"?
2. What could be a practical present-day equivalent of the Deuteronomy advice for reminders that we are God's people?

IF WE BUILD ON THE ROCK OF CHRIST, WHAT WILL OUR LIVES BE LIKE?

BUILDING ON ROCK

WHAT KIND OF BUILDING?

We're talking about lives, here.

WHAT KIND OF ROCK?

Faith in Jesus and his teaching. Not just hearing what he says, but acting on it as well.

YOU MEAN BRICKLAYING RATHER THAN JUST LOOKING AT THE PLANS?

Exactly. Sometimes we can let the words go in one ear and out of the other on Sunday. Jesus is saying that what we hear on Sundays should show on Mondays.

PLANS FOR CONSTRUCTION OF THE _____ LIFE!

YEARLY LEVEL

WEEKLY LEVEL

DAILY LEVEL

GROUND LEVEL
FOUNDATION STRUCTURE

HOW CAN WE DO IT, THOUGH? ROMANS 3:21-25, 28

DRAW THE PLANS OF YOUR LIFE BUILDING.

NAME THE CONSTRUCTION MATERIALS-THINGS LIKE ➡ WORSHIP SERVICE PRAYER BIBLE READING

AND MAKE IT QUITE DETAILED.

O GOD, THE STRENGTH OF ALL WHO PUT THEIR TRUST IN YOU, WE KNOW THAT, BEING HUMAN, WE CAN DO NO GOOD THING WITHOUT YOU. WE ASK YOU TO GIVE US YOUR GIFT OF GRACE, SO THAT WE CAN LIVE LIVES THAT ARE PLEASING TO YOU. —AMEN—

Tenth Sunday in Ordinary Time

Thought for the day

Jesus' life of healing and compassion acts out God's desire for mercy rather than empty sacrifice.

Readings

Hosea 6:3–6
Romans 4:18–25
Matthew 9:9–13

Aim: To explore the contrast between Jesus showing God's mercy and compassion, and the Pharisees' empty ritual and hypocrisy.

Starter

Which is the truth? On separate pieces of card, write out a number of words with various possible meanings. Read out all three possible definitions. They have to decide which one sounds most likely. Here are some examples to give you the idea:

BASTE: (a) to cover paper with glue; (b) to pour liquid over cooking food; (c) to sing in a low voice

IRE: (a) happiness; (b) misery; (c) anger

DAMASK: (a) a kind of fabric; (b) a pale color; (c) a kind of deer

LYRE: (a) someone who does not tell the truth; (b) a stringed instrument; (c) a wind instrument

Teaching

Ring a bell. In that game we were trying to work out which meaning rang true. God is concerned that our worship rings true, that what happens in our weekly services expresses the loving way we have been trying to live during the rest of the week. Look together at what God had said about this through the prophet Hosea, reading Hosea 6:3 and 6.

Explain how the Pharisees had become so enthusiastic about doing all the rituals of worship that these details had become far more important to them than the real work of giving honor and reverent worship to the loving God. Read the first part of today's gospel, and stop at the end of verse 10. What do they think about Jesus' behavior here? Was he right to be associating with people like this, or should he be avoiding them?

Now read verse 11. How would they answer this question from the Pharisees? Why do they think Jesus eats with tax collectors and "sinners"?

Finally read about the way Jesus responds to them, in verses 12–13, picking up on the quotation from the prophet Hosea and comparing it with their own ideas.

Praying

I'm coming back to the heart of worship
and it's all about you, all about you, Jesus.
I'm sorry, Lord, for the thing I've made it
when it's all about you, it's all about you, Jesus.

(From a song by Matt Redman
© Copyright 1997 Kingsway's Thankyou Music/EMI Christian Music Publishing)

Activities

On the activity sheet there is a role-play to try, based on the gospel reading, to bring out the feelings and attitudes behind the Pharisees' questions and Jesus' response to them, and there is space to plan a prayer vigil for the church on a matter of real social concern which they want to see addressed.

Discussion starters

1. How does ritual of any kind (or absence of it), originally a genuine expression of worship, sometimes turn into an empty shell, and how can we avoid it happening?

2. What assumptions does Jesus question in the call of Matthew?

Notes

3 PHARISEES IN A HUDDLE

ELIAS, EBENEZER AND ERIC

Elias	Calls himself a prophet! Huh – some prophet. Just look at him, laughing, enjoying himself.
Ebenezer	Yeah, not exactly the best company for a prophet, is it? Tax collectors, prostitutes . . .
Eric	Disgraceful. He obviously feels at home with them. Obviously one of them at heart.
Elias	Don't you think it's our duty – in love, of course – to tell him what bad publicity it'll get him?
Ebenezer	Yes, he ought to be upholding God's values, not messing with this lot! Shall we tackle him?
All	You're on!
	(They walk across and come back furious)
Eric	Incredible! Preposterous!
Elias	Sinister, if you ask me – and insulting!
Ebenezer	What have doctors got to do with it? These people are bad, not ill.
Eric	Standards'll start slipping, you mark my words.
Elias	Who does he think he is, for heaven's sake? Messiah himself?
Ebenezer	Fine thing that would be, if the Messiah turned out to be someone who loved sinners! What about the righteous?
Eric and Elias	Like us?
Ebenezer	Exactly.

EMPTY HABIT v. REAL WORSHIP

WHAT'S THE SCORE? Empty habit: nil – real worship: lots. There isn't any point in empty habit but real worship is a different matter.

WHAT DO YOU MEAN BY 'EMPTY HABIT'? GOING TO CHURCH AND PRAYING EACH DAY IS A GOOD HABIT, ISN'T IT? Yes, it certainly is. The nil score comes when we spend the week ignoring other people's needs and thinking only of ourselves, and then join in the hymns and prayers as if we've been living compassionately.

SO IT'S LIKE BEING TWO-FACED WITH GOD?

That's right. And God wants our worship and lives to be on the same team.

PRAYER VIGIL

TO PRAY FOR:

STYLE OF VIGIL: (CANDLES? MAPS? SILENCE? MUSIC?)

TIME AND DATE:

PUBLICITY: (MESSAGE ON HAND OUT? CHURCH MAG? LOCAL PAPERS?)

WHO DOES WHAT:

I'M COMING BACK TO THE HEART
OF WORSHIP AND IT'S ALL ABOUT YOU,
ALL ABOUT YOU, JESUS.
I'M SORRY, LORD, FOR THE THING
I'VE MADE IT
WHEN IT'S ALL ABOUT YOU,
IT'S ALL ABOUT YOU, JESUS.

(From a song by Matt Redman
© Copyright 1997 Kingsway's Thankyou Music/
EMI Christian Music Publishing.)

Eleventh Sunday in Ordinary Time

Thought for the day

Jesus sends his ambassadors out to proclaim God's kingdom and bring hope and peace of mind to the harassed and lost in every age.

Readings

Exodus 19:2–6
Romans 5:6–11
Matthew 9:36—10:8

Aim: To look at the sending-out of the twelve and its relevance for contemporary mission.

Starter

String up a length of washing line with clothespins on it. Have a chart with everyone's name on, and let each person take a turn at collecting the clothespins one-handed. The aim is to hold as many clothespins as possible in that one hand. This score can be entered against the names. The prize for the winner? A clothespin.

Teaching

First, read the passage from Exodus. Explain how Moses went back to his people with these words, how the people agreed to do what the Lord had said, but then didn't do what they said they would do. Talk about the problems that humans have of being unable to pull ourselves up by our own bootlaces. We can't save ourselves, but now Jesus has done for us what we could never do ourselves. Read Romans 5:6–11 to see how Paul explains this.

Go over with them the fact that Jesus needed to train a small team of people to carry on the work of spreading this good news, so that everyone in the world can benefit from it, and live their lives in a state of inner peace instead of turmoil and being harassed all the time. How many disciples (students) did he choose? Twelve. Do we know their names? Collect as many as they know and supply the rest. Today we are going to read about the time when Jesus sent these twelve out on mission.

Read today's gospel (Matthew 9:36—10:8). Talk together about how they were to go first to the "lost sheep of Israel" (link this with the Exodus reading), and how having few possessions and living simply they could act out the message of trusting in God. The principle of living simply—so that you are available to "travel light" wherever God calls you, and have more time for people—still

holds true today. The Church is still called to go out, without lots of wealth or power, and preach the good news and bring God's wholeness to people.

Does the church do this well, partly, or hardly at all?

Praying

This is a prayer of Saint Francis.

Lord, make me an instrument of your peace.
Where there is hatred let me sow love;
where there is injury, pardon;
where there is despair, hope;
and where there is sadness, joy.
Divine Master, grant that I may seek
not so much to be consoled as to console,
to be understood, as to understand,
to be loved, as to love.
For it is in giving that we receive,
it is in pardoning that we are pardoned,
and in dying that we are born to eternal life.

Activities

On the activity sheet there is some information about Saint Francis, who was particularly struck by today's gospel, and they are encouraged to question some of our assumptions about possessions and lifestyle.

Discussion starters

1. Is it foolish to talk about rejoicing and suffering in the same breath?

2. How would you interpret Jesus' instructions to the twelve for workers in the harvest today?

Notes

OF COURSE, YOU'LL WANT A JOB THAT GIVES A GOOD INCOME.

IF YOU DON'T PUSH, YOU DON'T GET ANYWHERE IN THIS LIFE.

LIVING SIMPLY JUST ISN'T POSSIBLE ANY MORE. YOU'D BE COMPLETELY OUT OF TOUCH.

LET'S FACE IT, WHAT YOU ARE WORTH IS HOW GOOD YOU LOOK.

OFF YOU GO!

WHO? Jesus was sending off his twelve disciples.

WHAT FOR?
So they could spread through the towns and villages and tell people the kingdom of God was close.

WHY MIGHT ANYONE BELIEVE THAT? MOST PEOPLE WOULD NEED TO SEE SOME SIGNS TO BACK UP THE CLAIM.
True. So they were given the power and authority to heal the sick, raise the dead, cleanse the lepers and drive out demons.

WOW!
Actually, God needs some workers now, if you're interested.

LORD, MAKE ME AN INSTRUMENT OF YOUR PEACE. WHERE THERE IS HATRED LET ME SOW LOVE; WHERE THERE IS INJURY, PARDON; WHERE THERE IS DESPAIR, HOPE; AND WHERE THERE IS SADNESS, JOY; DIVINE MASTER, GRANT THAT I MAY SEEK NOT SO MUCH TO BE CONSOLED AS TO CONSOLE, TO BE UNDERSTOOD, AS TO UNDERSTAND, TO BE LOVED, AS TO LOVE. FOR IT IS IN GIVING THAT WE RECEIVE, IT IS IN PARDONING THAT WE ARE PARDONED, AND IN DYING THAT WE ARE BORN TO ETERNAL LIFE.

A prayer of Saint Francis

SAINT FRANCIS OF ASSISI (ITALY)

BORN: Around 1181 – we don't know exactly.

BACKGROUND: Wealthy, fun loving, adventurous.

MOMENT OF TRUTH: He sensed God asking him to rebuild his ruined church, and took that to mean the tumble-down building he was in. He ended up building up the Church of God.

BEST BIBLE REFERENCE: Matthew 10:9-10.

LIFE STYLE: Very simple and basic. He and his group of 'brothers' walked about listening, loving, preaching, helping.

FOOD: Begging-bowl contents.

STATE OF MIND AND SPIRIT: Full of joy and humility, love and hope.

Twelfth Sunday in Ordinary Time

Thought for the day

When we are willing to take up our cross with Jesus we will also know his risen life.

Readings

Jeremiah 20:10–13
Romans 5:12–15
Matthew 10:26–33

Aim: To look at what it means to put God first in our lives.

Starter

Prepare fourteen sheets of paper as shown below, and arrange them in the right grid but the wrong order. They have to rearrange the letters by sliding the sheets, one move at a time, like those interlocking tiles puzzles. If it gets too frustrating they can simply arrange them by the number guide so that they end up with the correct message.

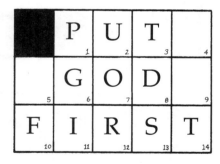

Teaching

Talk about how difficult it can be to get things in the right order of importance in our lives, and how getting the wrong order in life can be a messy business (like opening your bottle of ketchup before shaking it). More seriously, wars can cause a vast number of people to suffer, all because greed or power is a top priority rather than cooperation and sharing.

Read Matthew 10:26–33, to discover what Jesus has to say about what is important, and which things we should take most seriously. Notice how for God all our details—even the number of hairs on our head!—are very important because to him we are so precious. That's why he was willing to go through anything for us, even a tortured death. If Jesus is worth following at all, he is worth following closely, and to do that we really do need to put him first in our lives.

Look at the passage from Romans 5 to see how following Jesus through death to sin into resurrection life we will be dead to some things and alive to others. Some things will no longer have their hold of importance (like what?), and others will become more and more important to us (like what?).

Praying

True and living God,
I want to put you first in my life
so that all the rest can follow.
I want everything I think and do and say
to express what I know to be true:
that you are the living God
in whom I live and move and have my being.

Activities

On the activity sheet there is an interview with someone who has taken up cave exploring, so that they can see how taking up some things seriously affects the way you organize your life. This then opens up the practical implications of being a follower of Christ.

Discussion starters

1. Jesus says that what we hear from him in whispers, we are to proclaim from the housetops. What practical ways are there of doing this?

2. Jesus talks as if our Christian faith will be obvious to people. Is it? Or do we prefer to say what people want to hear, in case we upset them?

Notes

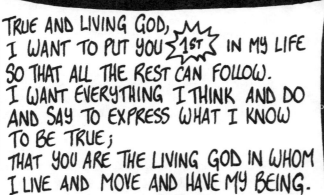

TRUE AND LIVING GOD,
I WANT TO PUT YOU 1ST IN MY LIFE
SO THAT ALL THE REST CAN FOLLOW.
I WANT EVERYTHING I THINK AND DO
AND SAY TO EXPRESS WHAT I KNOW
TO BE TRUE;
THAT YOU ARE THE LIVING GOD IN WHOM
I LIVE AND MOVE AND HAVE MY BEING.

COMMITTED TO CAVING

No. 1 – GOD

BUT WHAT ABOUT MY FAMILY AND FRIENDS?

Think of it this way. God is the source of all love. Your family and friends aren't. If you put God first, there'll be plenty of love from him to reach out to everyone else. But if you put people first, you'll miss out.

I SEE. IT'S NOT REJECTING OTHER PEOPLE TO BECOME A HOLY FREAK – IT'S ACTUALLY GETTING PRIORITIES RIGHT SO YOU'VE GOT MORE LOVE TO GIVE?

That's right. God doesn't chain us up – he sets us free!

Interviewer	Hello, Alan. We're standing here waist-deep in dark, cold water, in this cramped tunnel under the ground. We're wet and filthy. What is it that you like so much about caving?
Alan	Yes, I know it's uncomfortable, but I love caving! Just look up at those incredible stalactites over your head – spectacular! And you'd never see them unless you came caving. And I love the challenge of the rock, and getting through some of those narrow gaps. It's like being inside a great body – the body of our planet.
Interviewer	How much of your time gets taken up with caving, Alan?
Alan	Oh, it's a huge commitment, really. Keeping fit, checking equipment, travelling and so on. I live it, more than do it, if you know what I mean.
Interviewer	Are you ever scared?
Alan	Of course I am. But that's all part of the fun!
Interviewer	How much further before we're out in the open again?
Alan	Just another couple of hours.

HOW COMMITTED AM I TO CHRIST?

ENOUGH TO AFFECT THE WAY I LIVE?

Thirteenth Sunday in Ordinary Time

Thought for the day

As Christ's people we are no longer slaves to sin, but available for righteousness.

Readings

2 Kings 4:8–11, 14–16
Romans 6:3–4, 8–11
Matthew 10:37–42

Aim: To look at how we can offer ourselves either to sin for evil or to God for righteousness.

Starter

Sit in a circle and pass around a knife or a stone, with each person describing a way it could be used.

Teaching

Just as stones and knives can be used either for good or evil, so can we humans. We'll look first at how our voices can be used. Think of an example of this, perhaps from current news of lies in public places of power, or an ongoing concern such as tobacco promotion, or telemarketing sales pressure.

But it is not just our voices. What about other parts of our bodies which can be offered either to sin as an instrument for evil, or to God as an instrument for good? Do we want to offer some parts of our body to God but keep some bits back for sin? How can we use hands, ears, feet, our gifts, our education and our sexuality for good? How you talk about this will depend very much on the age and culture of your group, but it is an excellent opportunity to address life issues which need to be talked through in the Christian context. Try to cultivate an atmosphere of trust, where real concerns can be raised without embarrassment.

Finally look at the gospel for today, which reinforces God's recognition of every act of kindness and response to his love, however small or hidden.

Praying

Forth in thy name, O Lord, I go,
my daily labor to pursue;
thee, only thee, resolved to know
in all I think or speak or do.

Activities

There is opportunity on the activity sheet to define the difference between wages and a free gift, so they can see how "slavery to righteousness" is actually a freely given response to a personal free gift of grace. There is also a puzzle which helps reinforce the words of the gospel.

Discussion starters

1. If we think of ourselves as dead to sin and alive to God, how will we react in times of temptation, and when we are despised or ridiculed for our faith?

2. Obviously God wants us to love the people in our families, so how can we expect them to take second place to God in our lives, especially if they themselves are not believers?

Notes

78

THIS IS NOT A CIRCULAR

WAGES ARE...

WHAT'S THE DIFFERENCE?

A GIFT IS...

FROM SLAVERY TO RIGHTEOUSNESS

IF YOU'RE A SLAVE TO SIN, IS THE SIN STILL YOUR FAULT?

Yes. Being a slave to sin means you are locked into wrong attitudes and so behave selfishly whenever there is a choice. No one else chooses for you, so the sin is your fault.

BUT IT'S SO HARD TO BE UNSELFISH.

I know. That's why Jesus came and broke the hold sin has over us when he died on the cross. We can have his life and power in us to fight sin with.

IS IT EXPENSIVE?

It cost Jesus his life, but he gives it to us as a free gift.

Q: IF AN UNCLE GAVE YOU $10,000 WOULD YOU BE PLEASED?

| YES | NO |

Q: WOULD YOU WANT TO THANK HIM?

| YES | NO |

Q: SUPPOSE WHEN YOU THANKED HIM, HE TOLD YOU THAT YOU COULD THANK HIM BEST BY MAKING GOOD USE OF THE GIFT. WOULD YOU GO AWAY AND

- SPEND IT ALL ON YOURSELF? ☐
- THINK CAREFULLY ABOUT WISE SPENDING? ☐
- GIVE IT ALL AWAY? ☐
- TRY TO SPEND IT IN A WAY THAT WOULD PLEASE BOTH HIM AND YOU? ☐

FORTH IN THY NAME, O LORD, I GO,
MY DAILY LABOUR TO PURSUE;
THEE, ONLY THEE,
RESOLVED TO KNOW
IN ALL I THINK
OR SPEAK
OR DO.

WE CAN SHOW GOD OUR THANKS NOT ONLY IN WORDS BUT IN OUR LIVES AS WELL.

Fourteenth Sunday in Ordinary Time

Thought for the day

To all who are weary with carrying heavy burdens in life, Jesus offers rest for our souls and unthreatening relief.

Readings

Zechariah 9:9–10
Romans 8:9, 11–13
Matthew 11:25–30

Aim: To look at how we need to be childlike to accept God's love, but not childish.

Starter

Animal, plant, fruit. In a circle someone starts by saying, "If this person were an animal they would be a ...; if they were a plant they would be a...; and if they were a fruit they would be a..." Then everyone has to guess who it is. You can either stick to the people in the group for this, or have particular categories such as singers, sports personalities or film stars.

Teaching

We were able to work out some of those (or not, as the case may be!) because the animals, plants and fruit were chosen to sum up what the particular person is like. In the time that the book of Zechariah was written, certain animals had certain images that the people would relate to. A horse, for instance, was a symbol of war and power, and a donkey was a symbol of peace and humility. Read the passage from Zechariah, noticing how the image of a donkey is used, and what idea is being put across by this about the promised Messianic king. Remind them of how Jesus chose to enter Jerusalem many years later, so they can see the connection.

Look at the qualities of God which are listed in Psalm 144, and notice how these link up with the expected Messiah and Jesus riding into Jerusalem. At this point also read Matthew 11:28–30, as this, too, expresses those same qualities in action. (It is a passage that they could learn by heart to have with them at all times.)

Praying

The Lord is gracious and compassionate,
slow to anger and rich in love.

The Lord is good to all;
he has compassion on all he has made.
My mouth will speak in praise of the Lord.
Let every creature praise his holy name
forever and ever.

(From Psalm 145)

Activities

On the activity sheet there are animals as symbols associated with God to think about, and they will need dictionaries to look at the difference between "childish" and "childlike." There is also some help with learning Matthew 11:28 by heart, for which they will need a few balloons.

Discussion starters

1. When Jesus chose to enter Jerusalem on a donkey, what was he trying to show the people of Israel?

2. What is the difference between childish and childlike behavior, and why does being childlike make it possible for us to respond to God's wisdom?

Notes

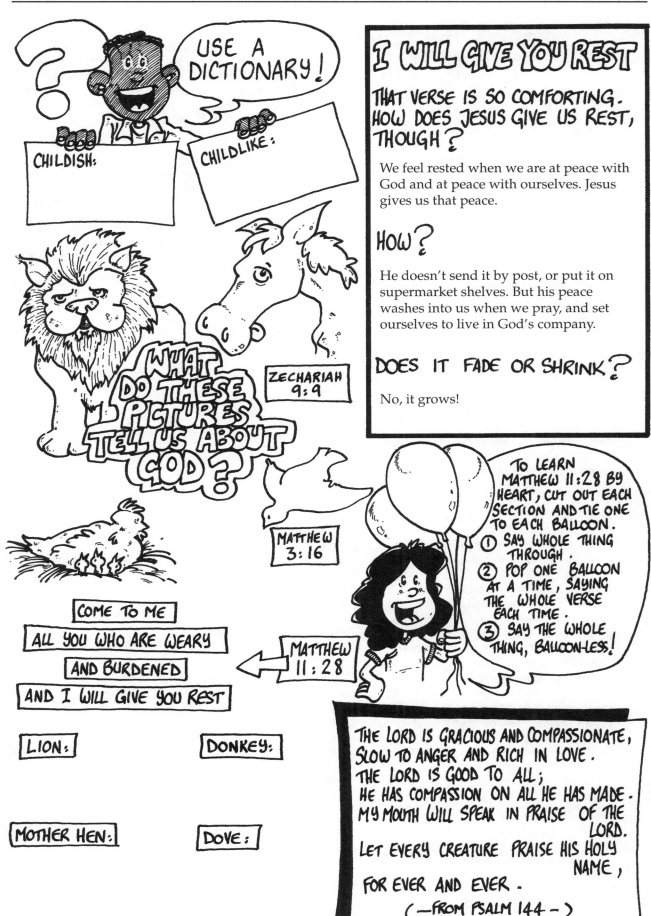

USE A DICTIONARY!

CHILDISH:

CHILDLIKE:

I WILL GIVE YOU REST

THAT VERSE IS SO COMFORTING. HOW DOES JESUS GIVE US REST, THOUGH?

We feel rested when we are at peace with God and at peace with ourselves. Jesus gives us that peace.

HOW?

He doesn't send it by post, or put it on supermarket shelves. But his peace washes into us when we pray, and set ourselves to live in God's company.

DOES IT FADE OR SHRINK?

No, it grows!

WHAT DO THESE PICTURES TELL US ABOUT GOD?

ZECHARIAH 9:9

MATTHEW 3:16

TO LEARN MATTHEW 11:28 BY HEART, CUT OUT EACH SECTION AND TIE ONE TO EACH BALLOON.
① SAY WHOLE THING THROUGH.
② POP ONE BALLOON AT A TIME, SAYING THE WHOLE VERSE EACH TIME.
③ SAY THE WHOLE THING, BALLOON-LESS!

COME TO ME
ALL YOU WHO ARE WEARY
AND BURDENED
AND I WILL GIVE YOU REST

MATTHEW 11:28

LION: DONKEY:

MOTHER HEN: DOVE:

THE LORD IS GRACIOUS AND COMPASSIONATE, SLOW TO ANGER AND RICH IN LOVE.
THE LORD IS GOOD TO ALL;
HE HAS COMPASSION ON ALL HE HAS MADE.
MY MOUTH WILL SPEAK IN PRAISE OF THE LORD.
LET EVERY CREATURE PRAISE HIS HOLY NAME,
FOR EVER AND EVER.
(—FROM PSALM 144 —)

Fifteenth Sunday in Ordinary Time

Thought for the day

Seed of God's word, sown in good soil, watered by his rain and warmed by his sunlight, produces a good crop of spiritual fruit.

Readings

Isaiah 55:10–11
Romans 8:18–23
Matthew 13:1–23

Aim: To explore the meaning of the parable of the growing seed, and its relevance to their own life.

Starter

Stage a quick *music jury game*, playing snippets of current releases, and asking each person to respond either with either a noise maker or a whoopee cushion, as appropriate.

Teaching

Point out that we all respond differently to particular music, and to everything in life, including one another. (Which is just as well, or we'd all be fighting for the same partner!) Today we are going to be looking at a parable Jesus told which is really about how we respond to God. The scene is set for us in a passage from Isaiah, which we will look at first.

Read Isaiah 55:10-11 together, picking up on the way the rain comes down, does its job and then goes back to the clouds. The job only gets done because the earth is able and ready to receive the rain and use it. (They may have come across the term "humus," whose earthy connections are important in the word "humility." Humility is rather like being earth, which is open to the sky.)

Before you look at Jesus' parable in Matthew 13, recap on what a parable is—a story with a hidden, deep meaning. Then read Matthew 13:1–9. Brainstorm about the possible meaning, keeping track of the ideas on a sheet of paper, with the main images listed: sower, seed, stony path, rock, thorns and good soil, before reading the next section of the gospel, which is the interpretation (Matthew 13:18–23).

Praying

True and living God,
you alone have the word of life
that I need.
All I am interested in is the real truth.
And that's you.

Activities

There is an opportunity on the activity sheet to record some of the points made in the discussion, and take these into a practical understanding of what various possible responses will mean in their lives. This may well lead into intercessory prayer for people they know and are concerned about.

Discussion starters

1. What makes some people more receptive to the word of God than others? Is it outside our control, or to do with our chosen attitudes and priorities?

2. Is it easier to believe in a creative sustaining God when we are in a rural setting, living with a rural economy? Is God relevant in the urban sprawl?

Notes

SOWER

SEED SOWN

SEED ON STONY PATH

SEED ON ROCK

SEED AMONG THORNS

SEED IN GOOD SOIL

A SOWER SOWED THE SEED

I THINK I AM SOMETIMES ONE KIND OF GROUND, SOMETIMES ANOTHER. THERE ARE TIMES I LISTEN AND TIMES I DON'T.

I reckon that's true for all of us. But we only have to be receptive earth. The growing is God's business.

YOU MEAN THERE'S NO POINT IN TRYING TO GROW?

There's no point in trying on our own. All we have to do is let God into our lives, and he'll do the rest within us.

CAN ANYONE END UP WITH A BIG CROP, THEN?

Yes. No qualifications needed, apart from being human and open to God.

...AND WHAT ABOUT US?

WHAT KIND OF THINGS STOP US HEARING THE GOSPEL PROPERLY?

STONY PATH →

ROCKY GROUND →

AMONG THORNS →

WHAT KIND OF THINGS MAKE FOR GOOD, WELL-PREPARED EARTH WHERE THE SEED CAN GROW?

WHAT OUR CHURCH COULD DO

WHAT OUR FRIENDS AND FAMILY COULD DO

TRUE AND LIVING GOD, YOU ALONE HAVE THE WORD OF LIFE THAT I NEED. ALL I AM INTERESTED IN IS THE REAL TRUTH - AND THAT'S YOU.

Sixteenth Sunday in Ordinary Time

Thought for the day

God's justice is always blended with mercy and loving kindness, so that we have real hope.

Readings

Wisdom 12:13, 16–19
Romans 8:26–27
Matthew 13:24–43

Aim: To know that God's nature is to be both just and merciful.

Starter

Give out a number of crimes, and decide on appropriate punishments for them. Here are some crime ideas:

- Taking the rest of a chocolate cracker pack that had only had two crackers previously eaten.
- Borrowing a favorite sweater and getting a mark on it.
- Copying your essay and getting a higher mark for it than it originally got.
- Playing baseball in the street and accidentally breaking a neighbor's stained-glass window.

Teaching

If you are found guilty in a court, a punishment has to be decided on which is fair and just. Today we are looking at where our desire to be fair comes from.

First read the passage from Wisdom. What has the writer discovered about God's nature? That he is both just and kind-hearted; that from his position of power and strength he chooses to act with lenience and mercy. If you have time read part of Psalm 86 as well, which echoes the realization of what God is like. Talk together about how people came to discover this, before they met Jesus. (Their own experiences of life, and the great events of the nation, such as the escape from Egypt.)

Since God is obviously just, how come there is so much evil and suffering in the world, much of which seems to go unchecked?

Then look at the parable Jesus told about the wheat and weeds, where, out of loving concern, the evil is allowed to continue at the moment, but it will not be so for ever. Ultimately, all that is good will be saved, and all that is evil will be destroyed. And in one sense, all of us belong to the kingdom now as well as then. God's people are called to

right injustice and "champion the unwanted" here and now.

Praying

Heaven shall not wait
for the poor to lose their patience,
the scorned to smile,
the despised to find a friend:
Jesus is Lord;
he has championed the unwanted;
in him injustice
confronts its timely end.

(From a song by John L. Bell and Graham Maule
© Copyright 1987 WGRG/GIA Publications, Inc.)

Activities

On the activity sheet there are instances of injustices which need righting, and space to plan possible action. They can also discover where they would stand on the "mercy line." Are there any suggestions for action within our families, or within the parish community?

Discussion starters

1. How would you answer someone who took all the terrible natural disasters as evidence that God is not merciful but cruel?

2. Can mercy sometimes prevent us from growing up and facing our responsibilities?

Notes

JUST AND FAIR

LIFE IS NEVER FAIR, IS IT?

For some people it is really unjust.

WHAT CAN WE DO ABOUT IT?

We can care. We can pray. We can push for changes.

MIGHT THAT MAKE US UNPOPULAR?

Probably.

I SUPPOSE THAT'S ALL PART OF BEING LIKE JESUS?

You've got it.

WHAT WE COULD DO AS A PARISH—
OUR CONCERN IS ...

WHAT WE THINK SHOULD HAPPEN IS ...

THIS IS HOW WE COULD HELP ...

HEAVEN SHALL NOT WAIT FOR THE POOR TO LOSE THEIR PATIENCE,
THE SCORNED TO SMILE, THE DESPISED TO FIND A FRIEND:
JESUS IS LORD; HE HAS CHAMPIONED THE UNWANTED;
IN HIM INJUSTICE CONFRONTS ITS TIMELY END.

(From a song by John L. Bell and Graham Maule,
© Copyright 1987 WGRG/GIA Publications Inc)

Seventeenth Sunday in Ordinary Time

Thought for the day

Jesus, the teacher, enables the ordinary, unlearned people to understand God's wisdom—the eternal laws of his Father's kingdom.

Readings

1 Kings 3:5, 7–12
Romans 8:28–30
Matthew 13:44–52

Aim: To look at how Jesus' teaching about God's wisdom is different from academic learning.

Starter

Mix a little yeast in with some flour and warm water, knead it and leave it in a warm place to see what happens.

Teaching

Together say the first part of the Lord's prayer, up to "your kingdom come." We may say these words every day, but what is it that we are praying for when we ask for the kingdom to come? Today we are going to look at some of the ways Jesus explained it to his followers.

Start with reading the gospel for today, with all the different pictures that are given to help us understand the nature of the kingdom of heaven, and list the images as they occur, or draw them, with the mustard plant and the yeasty flour grouped together, the treasure and the pearl together, and the fish in the net linked with the wheat and weeds from the previous week.

Talk together about the qualities of the kingdom which are being described in each case. (The way it grows and spreads, the way it is so precious and valuable that once we have found it everything else seems less important to us, and the way good and evil are allowed to continue alongside one another until the final gathering-in, when only what is good will last and be harvested.)

Look at the passage from 1 Kings 3, explaining first that Solomon was young and inexperienced, and about to embark on his reign. What does he ask God for? What is "wisdom?" (Having a heart that is skilled in listening to the real stories, so that we can distinguish good from evil, and understand what is really going on in a situation.) They will be able to see the link between this and what the Spirit enables us to do: God's wisdom is another way of describing God's Spirit, which leads us into all truth, in harmony with God's will.

Could you get a degree in wisdom? Could you write foolproof exam notes for it? No, it isn't a set of rules or a body of knowledge, but more like a relationship and an attitude to God and other people. The closer we get to God, the wiser we will become.

Praying

There is none like you,
no one else can touch my heart like you do.
I could search for all eternity long
and find there is none like you.

(From a song by Lenny LeBlanc
© Copyright 1991 Integrity's Hosanna! Music.)

Activities

On the activity sheet there is a script for a sketch which highlights the difficulty of discerning what is right and wrong, good and evil.

Discussion starters

1. Why do many people feel more comfortable learning about Jesus rather than entering into relationship with him?

2. Does it ring true to us to think of our faith as finding treasure in a field for which we dash off and sell everything we own?

Notes

CAN YOU MAKE A TRUE IMAGE OF THIS PICTURE?

ROMANS 8: 28-30

'THEY ARE THE ONES HE ☐☐☐☐☐ SPECIALLY LONG AGO AND INTENDED TO BECOME ☐☐☐☐ ☐☐☐☐☐☐ OF HIS ☐☐☐, SO THAT HIS SON MIGHT BE THE ☐☐☐☐☐☐ OF MANY ☐☐☐☐☐☐.'

GOD'S WISDOM

DOES THAT MEAN HOW CLEVER HE IS?

Not really. He is clever, of course, but wisdom is more than that. It's to do with seeing things as they really are, and knowing why.

HOW DO I GET IT?

Ask God for it. He has promised to give it to those who long for it.

WILL IT COME STRAIGHT AWAY?

It will grow, as you get closer to God.

THERE IS NONE LIKE YOU, NO ONE ELSE CAN TOUCH MY HEART LIKE YOU DO. I COULD SEARCH FOR ALL ETERNITY LONG AND FIND THERE IS NONE LIKE YOU.

(From a song by Lenny Le Blanc Copyright © 1991 Integrity's Hosanna! Music)

Harry Is it right to eat a Big Mac and fries?

Jane Of course, it's right – what are you talking about?

Harry Well, where does the beef come from?

Jane I dunno, maybe South America. You won't get Mad Cow Disease.

Harry But the rain forests have been cut back to clear loads of land for grazing, and all that's been lost just so we can eat our Big Mac.

Jane Well, this one's cooked already so it won't make much difference to the rain forest if we eat it, will it?

Harry Where do potatoes come from?

Jane Oh, come on, Harry, just eat it and stop worrying! You can't change the world.

Harry We can choose not to try.

Eighteenth Sunday in Ordinary Time

Thought for the day

God feeds all who come to him hungry, and we, as the Church, are expected to share in that work.

Readings

Isaiah 55:1–3
Romans 8:35, 37–39
Matthew 14:13–21

Aim: To explore what it means to be spiritually hungry and thirsty.

Starter

Give everyone a paper plate and ask them to draw on it a really satisfying meal they could eat when they're really hungry. Put the resulting drawings on the table like a feast and enjoy commenting on everyone's tastes.

Teaching

We all know what it means to be hungry for food because it happens to most of us most days. The hungrier you are, the less you are bothered by what you actually eat; as the body's urgency for food increases, anything will do. When your body has been without food for a long time the hunger stops being pleasant and becomes a real, desperate craving, and eventually a matter of life and death. That's how important food is.

This makes a very good picture to help us understand spiritual hunger and thirst. Read together the passage from Isaiah 55. What is the satisfying food and drink being offered here? Have a wrapped loaf of bread which lists the ingredients, and read these. Then read the list of "ingredients" of God in Psalm 145 to find out why this spiritual food is so satisfying.

Now look at today's gospel, with the feeding there, asking yourselves what feeding is going on, and who is hungry. Draw attention to the fact that the people had come here because they needed "feeding." Was Jesus able to feed those who had not chosen to come? How might those people eventually realize their hunger and get fed? (Think about the people who had been present at the feeding.) Why did Jesus bother to feed the people?

Think about the local area and any spiritual hunger they can see which is either not being fed or is being fed "junk food" rather than God's satisfying meals.

Praying

The King of love my shepherd is,
his goodness faileth never,
I nothing lack if I am his
and he is mine for ever.

(From Psalm 23)

Activities

On the activity sheet they can separate the spiritual junk food from proper, wholesome feeding, and look at signs of spiritual hunger and thirst in our society, thinking through ways the Church can get in touch with this and do the feeding it is called to do as the Body of Christ.

Discussion starters

1. Do the physically and emotionally well-fed have more difficulty recognizing spiritual hunger?

2. Are we, and how are we, as the Body of Christ, being broken to feed people God's spiritual food?

Notes

Nineteenth Sunday in Ordinary Time

Thought for the day
God is faithful to us through all the storms of life, yet our faith in God is so very small.

Readings
1 Kings 19:9, 11–13
Romans 9:1–5
Matthew 14:22–33

Aim: To look at that sinking feeling, and Jesus' rescue.

Starter
Provide some bowls of water and see how much cargo floating tubs can hold before they sink. This could be done in two teams, to see whose boat stays afloat longest.

Teaching
Today we are looking at a prophet with that sinking feeling. It's Elijah, who has done wonderful things which witness to the truth of the living God, and is at present exhausted and dejected and fearful. Read 1 Kings 19:9, 11–13, imagining how Elijah might have felt when at last he knew God's presence in the still small whisper.

Now look at today's gospel, jotting down the details under the following headings: Who? Where? When? What? How? Then think about "why." (What did Peter and the others learn from the incident? What new light does it throw on Jesus' identity?) Draw attention to the way you can often do things you would think impossible if you are following the instructions of a dynamic teacher or instructor. (Think of those TV documentaries about scary airplane rescues, where ordinary passengers need to take over the flight controls and are talked safely through landing by trusting the instructor in the control tower enough to do exactly as they say.) Jesus sees it all as a question of faith—the sort of faith which would make us quite naturally take an umbrella with us to pray for rain. This sort of faith expects real results, and, says Jesus, the results will happen. It's often our lack of real, practical believing in God which prevents his work from happening.

Praying
Lord, increase my faith
so that if you tell me
to step out more towards you,
I'll step out trusting you.

And if you tell me to stop, I'll stop,
and if you tell me to wait, I'll wait.
Lord, increase my faith;
Lord, increase my faith.

Activities
Stage an interview with Peter. Instructions and guidelines are provided on the activity sheet. Other activities encourage them to think through some of the reasons why people do get that "sinking" feeling, and how God helps us come to terms with it

Discussion starters
1. What kind of things build up our faith, and what knocks it about?

2. What can we learn from Elijah and Peter about God's reaction to people at the low and vulnerable points of life?

Notes

PETER, WHY DID YOU CLIMB OUT OF A BOAT IN THE MIDDLE OF A LAKE?

I KNOW IT SOUNDS CRAZY BUT... (THE STORM, SEEING JESUS, THINKING IT'S A GHOST, TO PROVE IT WASN'T)

COULD YOU WALK ON THE WATER?

YES! AS LONG AS I WAS ...

THEN WHAT HAPPENED?

I LOST IT! (...AFRAID OF THE STORMY WAVES, KNOWING I COULDN'T USUALLY DO IT, FEELING INSECURE...)

HOW COME YOU DIDN'T DROWN THEN?

IT WAS JESUS WHO SAVED ME. HE ...

OUTDOOR MIKE   ROCKY PETE

THAT SINKING FEELING

I GET THAT WHEN I SUDDENLY REALISE I CAN'T DO SOMETHING.

So do I. Peter did, too.

HOW COME PETER COULD WALK ON THE WATER?

He could cope while he kept his eyes and heart on Jesus. It was when he stopped trusting for a moment that he lost it.

IS THAT TRUE IN OUR LIVES AS WELL?

Yes. Jesus will get you through anything, if you keep your eyes on him.

HOW DO YOU KNOW?

I've done it. It works.

WHY DO WE GET THAT SINKING FEELING?

LORD, INCREASE MY FAITH SO THAT IF YOU TELL ME TO STEP OUT MORE TOWARDS YOU, I'LL STEP OUT TRUSTING YOU. AND IF YOU TELL ME TO STOP, I'LL STOP, AND IF YOU TELL ME TO WAIT, I'LL WAIT. LORD, INCREASE MY FAITH; LORD, INCREASE MY FAITH.

HINT: THINK OF ELIJAH

ANOTHER HINT: THINK OF PETER

HOW DOES GOD HELP?

AND HOW DOES HE USE US TO HELP?

Twentieth Sunday in Ordinary Time

Thought for the day

The good news of salvation is not limited to a particular group or nation but available for the whole world.

Readings

Isaiah 56:1, 6–7
Romans 11:13–15, 29–32
Matthew 15:21–28

Aim: To look at the implications of today's gospel about the healing of the daughter of the Canaanite woman.

Starter

Odd one out. Place a series of several objects down together and decide which are the odd ones out in each case. For instance, if you put down at random an umbrella, a pen, a CD and a chocolate bar, you may decide that the CD is the odd one out because it is more curved than straight; or that the chocolate bar is the odd one out as it is the only one that is edible. The more random the objects, the more brainwork there needs to be to find connections and misfits.

Teaching

Look first at today's gospel, Matthew 15:21–28. Draw attention to the parts of the reading which do not seem to fit in with the character of Jesus as we know it, or any areas that puzzle them. Initially they may well feel that Jesus was being unwelcoming and rude to the woman in her need. From where they are standing, what did it matter that she came from Canaan?

We need to put the story into context. Remind them of the original promise God made to Abraham because of his faith (Genesis 12:2–3), and how that led to the making of the chosen people. Jesus was born into this nation, and his mission was to gather up the chosen people and lead them, so that through them the rest of the world could be blessed. If Jesus had gone directly during his earthly ministry to preach to the gentiles, what would that have said to the Jewish people? Jesus was concerned to stay obedient to his calling. This woman is not part of that chosen people; in fact, she comes from a people traditionally held to be the enemy of God's ways.

So we find here a very human picture of Jesus, struggling with what is the right course of action in a very difficult situation. He doesn't immediately reject the woman, and we can imagine the conflict in his mind as he says nothing. The bit about not giving the children's food to the dogs is probably a proverb like "Charity begins at home," and so not nearly as rude as it sounds in translation. But the woman's reply makes Jesus realize that although she is not a "flesh and blood" descendant of Abraham, she is certainly his descendant through faith, and all doubt in his mind disappears about whether to include her in his ministry to the chosen people or not.

Praying

May God be merciful to us and bless us,
show us the light of his countenance and come to us.
Let your saving ways be known upon earth;
your saving health among all nations.
Let the peoples praise you, O God,
let all the peoples praise you.

(From Psalm 67)

Activities

There is help on the activity sheet for exploring Romans 11 in the light of today's teaching, and an activity to encourage them in thinking through our calling to continue spreading the gospel, with suggestions of opportunities for doing this in their lives.

Discussion starters

1. What have today's readings to teach us about those who have not yet been introduced to the one true living God?

2. Was Jesus just being narrow-minded when he declined to help the Canaanite woman, or very traditional, or was he making a deliberate teaching point here?

Notes

ROMANS 11

① DID GOD THROW OUT HIS CHOSEN PEOPLE WHEN THEY FAILED TO ACCEPT JESUS AS MESSIAH? (VERSE 1 – 2A) YES ☐ NO ☐

② DOES GOD EVER CHANGE HIS MIND ABOUT PEOPLE HE CALLS? (VERSE 29) YES ☐ NO ☐

③ ARE THE JEWS THE ONLY ONES TO DISOBEY GOD? (VERSE 32) YES ☐ NO ☐

④ WHAT DO WE RECEIVE FROM GOD WHEN WE KNOW WE HAVE BEEN DISOBEDIENT? FAITH ☐ MERCY ☐ PUNISHMENT ☐

⑤ WHO IS NOW RELYING ON GOD'S MERCY? THE JEWS ☐ THE GENTILES ☐ EVERYONE ☐

WHY NOT GENTILES TOO?

IT SEEMS RUDE OF JESUS NOT TO WANT TO HEAL THIS WOMAN'S DAUGHTER. WAS HE BEING RUDE?

Jesus knew he was called to bring the good news first to the Jewish people. The idea was that they would then spread the light through the world.

SO WHY DID HE CHANGE HIS MIND, AND HEAL HER?

He could see that, by her faith, she was a descendant of Abraham, even though she came from the enemy nation of Canaan.

HE SEEMS SURPRISED BY HER FAITH.

Yes, she had more faith than the chosen people of God.

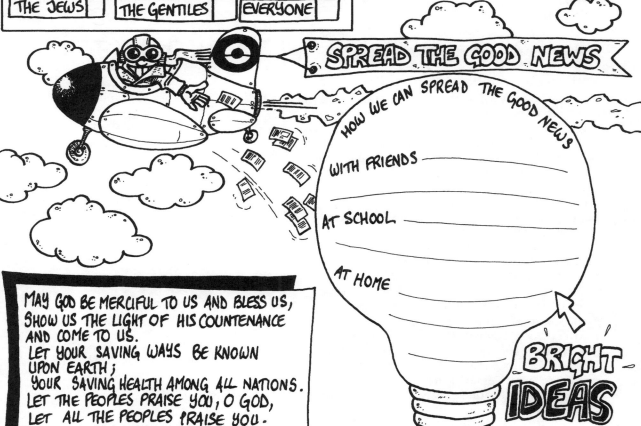

SPREAD THE GOOD NEWS

HOW WE CAN SPREAD THE GOOD NEWS

WITH FRIENDS _____

AT SCHOOL _____

AT HOME _____

BRIGHT IDEAS

MAY GOD BE MERCIFUL TO US AND BLESS US, SHOW US THE LIGHT OF HIS COUNTENANCE AND COME TO US.
LET YOUR SAVING WAYS BE KNOWN UPON EARTH;
YOUR SAVING HEALTH AMONG ALL NATIONS.
LET THE PEOPLES PRAISE YOU, O GOD,
LET ALL THE PEOPLES PRAISE YOU.
(— FROM PSALM 66 —)

Twenty-first Sunday in Ordinary Time

Thought for the day

The Church is the Body of Christ, built on strong rock of faith and energized by the living Breath of God.

Readings

Isaiah 22:15, 19–23
Romans 11:33–36
Matthew 16:13–20

Aim: To look at the Church in the light of its roots and heritage.

Starter

Who's who? They will need Bibles for this. Working in pairs, discover who's who from a list of clues. Here are some suggestions:

- this person killed his brother—Genesis 4:8
- this woman drove a tent peg through an army commander's head—Judges 4:21
- this person caused a great temple full of people to collapse—Judges 16:29–30
- this person was so excited to find Peter knocking at the door that she left him there outside—Acts 12:13–16
- this person escaped by being let down over the city wall in a basket—Acts 9:25

Teaching

Look first at today's gospel, up to verse 14, and see who people thought Jesus was. Why might they have thought he was John the Baptist or Elijah or one of the prophets? In what ways was he behaving like them? What reasons are there for thinking he wasn't any of these people?

Then look at what the disciples thought, and Simon said (15–16). What might have brought them to this conclusion? What had they seen Jesus doing which convinced them?

Now look at Jesus' response to Simon's reply (17–20). Notice Jesus' joy and excitement that Simon has finally gotten to the point of real faith which Jesus had been longing for. The new name he gives him to mark this event and prophesy Simon's leadership role in the church is often translated as "Rock," though in the Greek it has the sense of great boulder! The church is to be established on the firm bedrock of Jesus, the Christ, the Son of God, which Simon Peter has just confessed, and it will be led by the human Peter, with strong faith in that truth.

This is the first time "Church" is mentioned in the New Testament, and it must have come as quite a shock to the disciples, who had been thinking of a kingdom with a king on a throne, to hear that it was planned to be more like a community or society of equal people. It doesn't seem to be just earthly, either. Jesus sees it standing firm against all kinds of evil attack, from outside and in, being constantly renewed and revived through all the centuries, touching both heaven and earth.

And that is the same Church which we belong to now, in this parish, in this country!

Praying

Lord Jesus, you are the Christ,
the Son of the living God!
Revive your Church in our generation
so that the whole world benefits.

Activities

The teaching is reinforced on the activity sheet with an exploration of where the Church does show these important roots, and where today's readings
challenge us as church members.

Discussion starters

1. What do you think had helped Simon Peter realize the true identity of Jesus?

2. In what ways is the Church of today a real, living body?

Notes

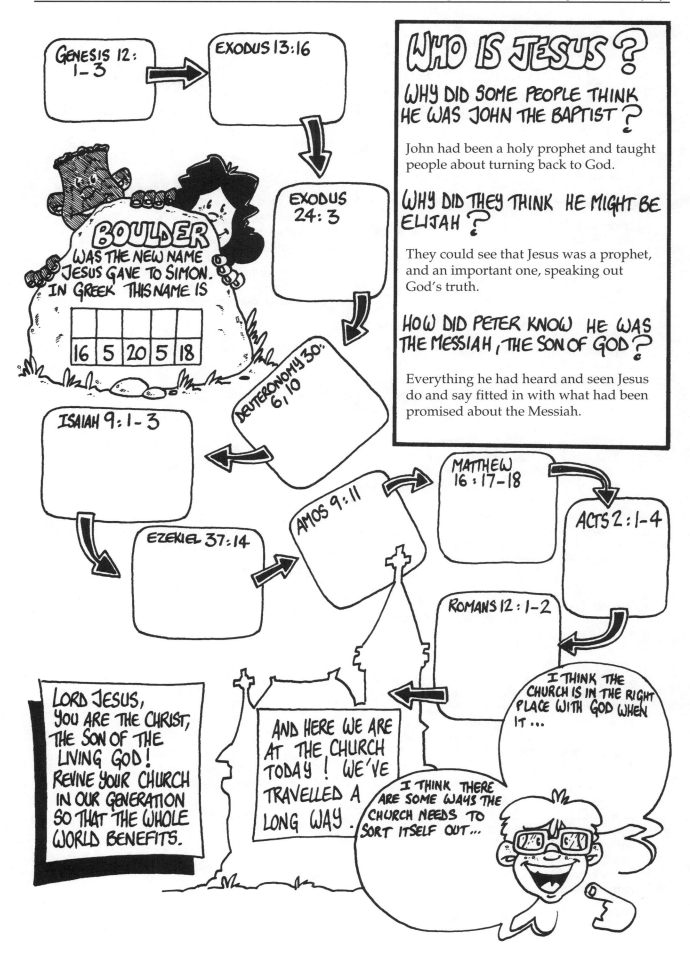

Twenty-second Sunday in Ordinary Time

Thought for the day
As Jesus prepares for the necessary suffering of the cross, he is tempted, through well-meaning friendship, to avoid it.

Readings
Jeremiah 20:7–9
Romans 12:1–2
Matthew 16:21–27

Aim: To look at why Jesus had to suffer and why Peter's advice was rejected.

Starter
Give out road maps and ask them to find a route to the state capital from their town which will avoid a busy suburb in the rush hour. (They will find this is virtually impossible without a vast detour!)

Teaching
Today we are looking at how some things have to be faced and can't be avoided, however much we would like to side-step them. First tell them about a prophet named Jeremiah, who never found it easy to be God's spokesman but knew that was his calling. Today's reading finds him full of doubts and fears, pouring his heart out to God. Do they ever feel like this? Is it OK to talk to God like this? Yes, it is! God wants us to come to him "real," wherever we happen to be. Part of prayer is working through our feelings of anger and resentment, with God who can help us with them.

Now read today's Psalm. See how God is always with us, as he would have been with Jeremiah. We are never expected to work on our own, but always with God to help us, and that eases the load.

Now look at today's gospel, where Jesus, in his human nature, is dreading and fearing the suffering of the cross, while at the same time, in his divine nature, he can see it as the glorious plan of salvation which will bring hope to the world. He can't afford to be tempted to side-step the suffering which is all part of the package.

Praying
Lord, my God,
may I love with sincerity,
hate what is evil
and cling to what is good.
May I be joyful in hope,
patient in affliction

and faithful in prayer. Amen.

Activities
On the activity sheet there is a short sketch to read or act out, which looks at our willingness to offer ourselves but our surprise at being expected to put up with some costly giving as part of the deal. Also they are encouraged to pray for those having doubts and misgivings, and those going through a time of testing.

Discussion starters
1. How can we ensure that our well-meaning friendship never becomes a stumbling block to another's spiritual growth?

2. Are we prepared to accept the cross God needs to lay on us, or are we trying to remain in control and choose our own?

Notes

LORD, MY GOD,
MAY I LOVE WITH SINCERITY,
HATE WHAT IS EVIL,
AND CLING TO WHAT IS GOOD.
MAY I BE JOYFUL IN HOPE,
PATIENT IN AFFLICTION
AND FAITHFUL IN PRAYER.
— AMEN —

TRUST ME TO VOLUNTEER!

IT HAS TO BE DONE

WHY COULDN'T JESUS AVOID THE SUFFERING OF THE CROSS?

There was no other way to show that his love for us is total and without limit. He had to be willing to give everything, including dignity and life.

IT MUST HAVE SCARED HIM.

Yes, it did. We know that when Peter suggested avoiding it, he was tempted to think Peter might be right. And in the garden of Gethsemane, Jesus was sweating blood at the thought of all the suffering ahead.

THANK HEAVENS JESUS HAD THE COURAGE TO GO THROUGH WITH IT!

It certainly proves he loves us!

Teacher	I wonder if I could have a couple of volunteers for running one of the side shows at the school fair?
Michael	I'll do it, sir!
Terry	So will I!
Teacher	Excellent. Thanks, Michael. Thanks, Terry. Meet me in the playground to set it up on Saturday afternoon, 2 o'clock.
Michael	Right, sir. We'll be there.
Terry	It should be fun.

* *

Julia	Let's have a go at throwing wet sponges at someone in the stocks now.
Pat	Good idea. Hey, those guys in the stocks look very familiar.
Julia and Pat	It's Michael and Terry! Come on, you two – smile! It's Saturday.
Michael	Huh. I didn't bargain for cold wet sponges all afternoon.
Pat	Here it comes, Terry! SPLAT!

25¢ A TURN

PRAY FOR THOSE...

BEING TEMPTED HAVING DOUBTS SUFFERING

LORD HAVE MERCY

Twenty-third Sunday in Ordinary Time

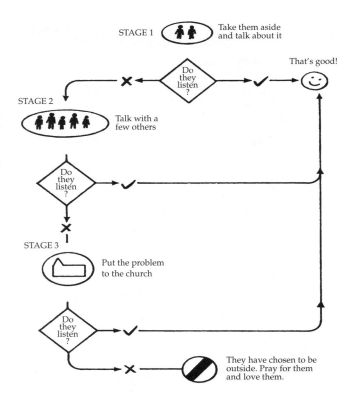

STAGE 1 — Take them aside and talk about it

Do they listen? — That's good!

STAGE 2 — Talk with a few others

Do they listen?

STAGE 3 — Put the problem to the church

Do they listen?

They have chosen to be outside. Pray for them and love them.

Thought for the day

It is our responsibility to encourage and uphold one another in living by the standard of real love.

Readings

Ezekiel 33:7–9
Romans 13:8–10
Matthew 18:15–20

Aim: To explore our responsibility as Christians to encourage and uphold one another.

Starter

Play "pick-up-sticks," using either the bought game, or drinking straws or sticks. Having tipped all the sticks on to a table, each person has to try and remove one without any of the others moving.

Teaching

What made it hard to move one stick on its own was that all the sticks were holding one another up. As Christians, we need to be holding one another up like that, in an interconnected heap of God's love and care, so that we can't easily be tempted away from living in God's promise.

Read the passage from Ezekiel 33. There are two important things to look at here:

1. If we don't warn people and encourage them to turn back to God when they are in the wrong place, we will be held responsible to God for them.

2. The last thing God wants is for people to perish, and he will always forgive; no one is ever a hopeless case.

It's a bit like those sticks again—if evil is trying to pull someone away, we need to start moving, supporting them so they are safe.

Now read today's gospel, with Jesus picking up on the teaching in Ezekiel and giving us guidelines for dealing with situations where people need to be approached about how they are behaving, or about wrong attitudes. Have the process drawn out like a program sequence (see illustration) and trace it through together.

Then look at the passage from Romans, to remind ourselves of what we are aiming at, and what those right attitudes are.

Praying

Lord God, give me understanding
to keep your law of love
so that I walk in the path of your commandments,
for that is what I really want to do.
Help us to encourage one another in living your way
and protect one another from falling.

Activities

The program sequence is shown on the activity sheet and this can be used as a basis for a role-play. Suggestions are given for this. They are also encouraged to put in place any practical ideas for mutual support, and their ideas may be valuable for the whole parish community.

Discussion starters

1. Why do we instinctively draw back from facing someone with their sin and talking through it with them? Should we have a special ministry for this, or is it everyone's concern?

2. Where does welcome and acceptance of the sinner turn into a lack of concern for their behavior which is damaging for them and the community?

Twenty-fourth Sunday in Ordinary Time

Thought for the day

Forgiving is a natural result of loving, so it is not an option for us but a command.

Readings

Sirach 27:30—28:7
Romans 14:7–9
Matthew 18:21–35

Aim: To look at what forgiving is and what it isn't.

Starter

Backwards. Ask each group to work out a series of actions, first doing them forwards and then in reverse, such as washing and drying up, or taking an exam.

Teaching

Today we are going to look at what forgiving is all about. Like our forward and reverse sequences, forgiving is rather like giving in reverse. In the Lord's Prayer we ask for God to give us our daily bread and to forgive, or take from us, our sin, rather as you can suck out the juice from an ice pop. Forgiveness is something we have to have done for us by the forgiver. We are completely dependent on their kindness and mercy, and if they choose not to forgive us, then we won't be forgiven by them. You can't force someone to forgive you.

Look at Matthew 18:21–22. How is Peter thinking of forgiveness if he feels seven times is quite enough? Probably from the point of view that we don't deserve to be treated badly by people that much, and shouldn't put up with it. Look at the first part of Jesus' story, up to verse 27. That is the true situation with each of us and God. We've had taken from us a debt which we had no hope of ever repaying, and out of love for us God chose to cancel that debt through the sacrifice of Jesus on the cross.

Now read on to verse 35. That's how small-minded we are when we fuss about forgiving other people. Our two great rules of life are to love God and love one another as ourselves. Loving leads us to want to forgive, so it follows that forgiving is not something we have a right to choose, according to circumstances, but something that, as Christians, we are required to do as part of the rule of love.

Praying

Give us today our daily bread
and for-give us our sins,
as we for-give those who sin against us.

Activities

On the activity sheet there are some situations to look at where forgiveness is costly, and examples of the differences between forgiving, forgetting and excusing.

Discussion starters

1. To "forgive and forget": how easy is it to do both?

2. If only God can forgive sins, how can we be expected to do it?

Notes

WHAT IS FORGIVING?

Forgiving is cancelling a debt. If someone has wronged you it's as if they are in debt to you. When you forgive them you let them off.

IS THAT EXCUSING THEM?

No. With forgiving, you both recognize that there is wrong done. You don't pretend it's OK. You are saying, 'I agree you have done wrong to me, but I still let you off.'

THAT'S HARD TO DO.

Yes, if you have been badly hurt it's very hard. But we have to do it all the same.

FORGETTING IS

EXCUSING IS

JAIL

FORGIVING IS

GIVE US TODAY
OUR DAILY BREAD
AND FOR-GIVE US OUR SINS
AS WE FOR-GIVE
THOSE WHO SIN
AGAINST US.

Twenty-fifth Sunday in Ordinary Time

Thought for the day

We have no right to be envious of the generosity and mercy God shows to others.

Readings

Isaiah 55:6–9
Philippians 1:20–24, 27
Matthew 20:1–16

Aim: To look at the nature of God's generosity.

Starter

In a circle pass around a twenty dollar bill (or a Monopoly equivalent). As it gets to each person they say how they would spend it if it was theirs, and next time around they say who or what they would give it to and why, if they were going to give it away.

Teaching

Look at the parable Jesus told in Matthew 20. It can be read as a group, with parts being taken by different voices. Had the workers agreed a fair wage before they started? Why were they grumbling, then? Point out that it was the owner's right to be generous with his money—and the all-day shift was not losing out. Jesus wanted his hearers to see that whether people came to faith early or late in life, God was simply overjoyed that they were saved. We don't earn our right to everlasting life in any case; new life is a freely given gift, and we shouldn't ever begrudge people having it, even if we feel we have worked harder for God or our church than they have.

Praying

Christ's is the world in which we move,
Christ's are the folk we're summoned to love,
Christ's is the voice which calls us to care,
and Christ is the one who meets us there.

(From a song by John L. Bell and Graham Maule
© Copyright 1989 WGRG/GIA Publications, Inc.)

Activities

The activity sheet looks at the significance of "the last shall be first and the first shall be last" and helps them think through ways of being generous in God's terms, without the limitations and parameters we usually fix in place.

Discussion starters

1. Are we happy to do God's work, or would we rather do our work, maintaining our control, and offer it to God complete?

2. Are we still expecting God to keep to our rules and guidelines? How can we avoid this in all our planning and church activities?

Notes

THE LAST SHALL BE FIRST AND THE FIRST SHALL BE LAST!

IF THAT'S SO, DOES THE ORDER THAT PEOPLE COME TO FAITH GREATLY MATTER?

| NOT AT ALL | VERY MUCH |

IF YOU SHARE GOD'S HOPE THAT ALL WILL BE SAVED, HOW WILL YOU FEEL ABOUT SOMEONE COMING TO FAITH AT THE VERY LAST MINUTE OF THEIR LIFE?

| DELIGHTED | ANNOYED |

THE BEST GIVER EVER

I KNOW GOD GIVES US LIFE, AND CREATION. HOW ELSE IS HE GENEROUS?

He always wants the best for us, so he is generous in his thinking as well as his giving.

IF HE WASN'T GENEROUS, WHAT WOULD HAPPEN TO US?

Well, we can't earn our way into heaven – we rely on the generous mercy of God to save us. So, if God wasn't generous, there would be no hope. But then, he wouldn't be God, and we wouldn't be either!

WE NEED TO BREAK THROUGH OUR BARRIERS OF GIVING

BUT NOT THOSE!

I WANT TO HELP THESE PEOPLE ...

THESE PEOPLE DESERVE MY FRIENDSHIP...

BUT NOT THOSE!

CHRIST'S IS THE WORLD IN WHICH WE MOVE,
CHRIST'S ARE THE FOLK WE'RE SUMMONED TO LOVE,
CHRIST'S IS THE VOICE WHICH CALLS US TO CARE,
AND CHRIST IS THE ONE WHO MEETS US THERE!

Twenty-sixth Sunday in Ordinary Time

Thought for the day

God longs for us to die to sin and live, but it has to be our choice, too.

Readings

Ezekiel 18:25–28
Philippians 2:1–11
Matthew 21:28–32

Aim: To look at our choices and their consequences.

Starter

Consequences. Pass around sheets of paper so that each line is added by a different person. If it's a long time since you played this, here are the sections, to refresh your memory:

1. Boy's name
2. Girl's name
3. Place
4. He said to her…
5. She said to him…
6. The consequence was…

Then all the versions are shared and enjoyed.

Teaching

Today we are looking at the choices we make, and the consequences of them. First read the passage from Ezekiel, where the prophet is speaking out God's concern for the people. Although God loves them and hopes they will turn to him, if they deliberately turn away then the terrible consequences will not be God's fault but their own. Think about some present-day examples, but also notice the important message that God doesn't want anyone to perish— he's not trying to catch us so we fail. Also, notice how it's our own responsibility that counts; we are not to blame for wrongs committed by anyone else against us.

Now read about Jesus' confrontation with the religious leaders. Use the parable of the two sons to see what Jesus was trying to show these leaders, and what they were refusing to hear.

In complete contrast, look at the beautiful words in Philippians about Jesus, so that we can all benefit from this amazing example of humility and chosen obedience. That can inspire us, and, as Paul says, Jesus promises us live-in help to make right choices in life.

Praying

Lord, may our attitude be the same
as that of Christ Jesus,
who, being in very nature God,
did not consider equality with God
something to be grasped,
but made himself nothing,
taking the very nature of a servant,
being made in human likeness
and being found in appearance as a man,
he humbled himself and became obedient to death—
even death on a cross!

Activities

The activity sheet includes a choices activity, and they are encouraged to think through the possible consequences of wrong and right choices. They could also work with music and mime to bring the Philippians reading to life and share this with the people in church.

Discussion starters

1. Does a loving and merciful nature mean that God will overlook all evil, or should we be looking at the prospect of judgment far more seriously than is fashionable?
2. Why did the religious leaders not recognize what God was doing? Can this still happen today?

Notes

LORD, MAY OUR ATTITUDE BE THE SAME
AS THAT OF CHRIST JESUS,
WHO BEING IN VERY NATURE GOD,
DID NOT CONSIDER EQUALITY WITH
GOD SOMETHING TO BE GRASPED,
BUT MADE HIMSELF NOTHING,
TAKING THE VERY NATURE OF A SERVANT,
BEING MADE IN HUMAN LIKENESS
AND BEING FOUND IN APPEARANCE
AS A MAN, HE HUMBLED HIMSELF
AND BECAME OBEDIENT TO DEATH –
EVEN DEATH ON A CROSS !

CHOICES

HOW ARE WE ABLE TO CHOOSE?

Our brains are able to see several possible routes. Our conscience tells us which is right and which is wrong. Our will enables us to make the choice.

WHY DIDN'T GOD MAKE US PROGRAMMED FOR RIGHT AND GOOD?

In a way we are – we can usually tell right from wrong, even if we don't choose wisely. But if we *had* to do right, we would be robots, not free humans, able to love by making 'self' take a back seat.

THE PERSON TO GO WITH?

THE MEAL?

DREAM ON!

THE FILM?

THE TRANSPORT?

POSSIBLE CONSEQUENCES?

EATING ALL YOUR EASTER EGGS AT ONCE

LYING ABOUT WHO YOU ARE ON THE PHONE TO

BORROWING WITHOUT ASKING

BOASTING ABOUT A SKILL YOU HAVEN'T GOT

ACTING A PART TO BE ACCEPTABLE TO YOUR 'FRIENDS'

HAVE A NICE EVENING !

Twenty-seventh Sunday in Ordinary Time

Thought for the day
God does everything possible for our spiritual growth and well-being, but still we can choose hostility and rejection.

Readings
Isaiah 5:1–7
Philippians 4:6–9
Matthew 21:33–43

Aim: To look at the vineyard stories and their meanings in context and for our own time and situation.

Starter
Make toffee apples. Push sticks into the apples and dip them into the toffee, which has been mixed beforehand and just needs the cooking. Alternatively, use melted chocolate for dipping. Leave them to harden on wax paper.

Teaching
Remind them of the situation Jesus was facing in last week's gospel, with the Scribes and Pharisees confronting him while he was teaching the people and demanding to be told by what authority he was doing so. Having told them through the parable of the two sons that they needed to get their act together and start putting their own words into action, Jesus now starts to tell them a story they would already know. (We are sometimes less threatened and more ready to listen to familiar things.)

First read the parable as it is in the Old Testament, in Isaiah. The "who's who" is also made clear here. They have just experienced the satisfaction of good fruit; God is saying he has lavished care on this vineyard, but it has only produced bad, disappointing spiritual fruit, and cannot avoid becoming overgrown and overrun with weeds. National misery is bound to come to a people who have rejected their God.

Then go on to the parable Jesus told the religious leaders, picking up on the similarities and the differences. (It is often helpful to people if these are noted in two columns.) Read up to verse 39. What do they think the message is now? Who is the owner, who are the farmers and the servants?

Once you have discussed this, look at the question Jesus asks, and the answer he gets (verses 40–43). Do you think the leaders realize that they are the farmers in the story? Jesus follows the parable with direct teaching, explaining their situation to them, and it hits them that Jesus was talking about them, but that didn't make them change their hearts—it only made them more determined than ever to get rid of this teacher.

Praying
Turn now, O God of hosts, look down from heaven;
behold and tend this vine,
preserve what your right hand has planted.
Restore us, O God of hosts;
show us the light of your countenance (face)
and we shall be saved.

(From Psalm 80)

Activities
On the activity sheet there are questions to answer about both "vineyard" stories.

Discussion starters
1. How might knowledge of the Isaiah parable enable those listening to Jesus to grasp the significance of his version?

2. Paul was also a Pharisee. How can we account for the astounding difference in outlook between the Pharisees in today's gospel and the letter to the Christians at Philippi?

Notes

WHO'S WHO?

IN THE ISAIAH PARABLE

THE OWNER ?
THE VINEYARD ?
THE PLANTED VINE ?
NO FRUIT/BAD FRUIT ?

IN THE PARABLE JESUS TOLD

THE KING ?
THE VINEYARD ?
THE PLANTED VINE ?
THE SERVANTS ?
THE LABOURERS ?
THE KING'S SON ?

FACING GOD'S TRUTH

WHY DID THE PHARISEES FIND IT SO HARD TO SEE WHAT THEY WERE DOING WRONG ?

We tend to ignore or reject truths we don't want to see.

BUT THEY KNEW THE LAW SO WELL.

Yes. In fact, they hugged it so tightly it couldn't breathe. When Jesus showed them what it was really like they thought of him as a threat instead of a savior.

PHILIPPIANS 4: 6-9

WRITE IN WHAT WE ARE TO FILL OUR MINDS WITH!

TURN NOW, O GOD OF HOSTS, LOOK DOWN FROM HEAVEN; BEHOLD AND TEND THIS VINE, PRESERVE WHAT YOUR RIGHT HAND HAS PLANTED. RESTORE US, O GOD OF HOSTS; SHOW US THE LIGHT OF YOUR COUNTENANCE AND WE SHALL BE SAVED.

(— FROM PSALM 79 —)

DICTIONARY

COUNTENANCE = FACE

Twenty-eighth Sunday in Ordinary Time

Thought for the day

We are all invited to God's wedding banquet, but in accepting we must allow the rags of our old life to be exchanged for the freely given robes of holiness and right living.

Readings

Isaiah 25:6–10
Philippians 4:12–14, 19–20
Matthew 22:1–14

Aim: To explore the implications of the wedding feast parable both for the people of Israel and the members of the Church.

Starter

Rules of the game. Give them a ball and a bucket. They are going to use these to invent the rules for a new game, and play it.

Teaching

In their game, as in all others, abiding by the rules is essential. If you choose to play any sport, it's understood that you will get sent off if you deliberately break the code laid down. Today one of Jesus' parables invites us to look at this in relation to the kingdom of God.

First read the Isaiah passage. It is full of praise and thanks, and also looking forward to a time of complete victory and joy. Then read the passage from Romans, with its rejoicing and security in God's love which helps us concentrate on all that is lovely, noble, right and good, even when there is great anxiety all around.

Now comes the parable of the wedding banquet in today's gospel. Place it in its context of Jesus speaking both generally to the people and also directing a particular, hidden message to the Pharisees who were out to destroy him. Explain the custom of giving out wedding garments from the palace to all guests; otherwise the full insult of the guest is not understood. Then, using one sheet headed "Pharisees" and the other "Riff-raff," jot down their ideas about the message in the parable for each.

Praying

You prepare a table for me
in the presence of my enemies;
you anoint my head with oil, and my cup overflows.
Surely goodness and mercy shall follow me
all the days of my life;
and I shall dwell in the house of the Lord for ever.

(From Psalm 23)

Activities

On the activity sheet they are encouraged to look at the symbolism of old and new "habits," and the difference between being expected to change on our own, and receiving the freely given grace which makes it possible. They also look at the kind of Pharisaic attitudes that are just as likely to happen now
as then.

Discussion starters

1. What does it say about a guest if he accepts the King's invitation but not his freely given new clothing of holiness?

2. Why do you think Jesus made it a wedding feast, rather than any other celebration?

Notes

Twenty-ninth Sunday in Ordinary Time

Thought for the day

All leaders and rulers are subject to the ultimate authority and power of God, the living truth.

Readings

Isaiah 45:1, 4–6
1 Thessalonians 1:1–5
Matthew 22:15–21

Aim: To look at issues of authority and leadership from a Christian perspective.

Starter

Give everyone some newspaper with which to make a hat in five minutes.

Teaching

The newsprint represents the events considered of world importance by the media, and they have made them into head-gear. Today we are going to look at those who head countries and states, and at how this fits in with God's authority.

First read the passage from Isaiah 45, where the prophet sees God's hand in the political events of time, with even other national leaders being used by the God they do not worship. The crucial sentence is "I am the Lord," and God's total authority is established clearly.

You could also look at the Thessalonians reading, which reinforces the understanding of God being the living truth.

Now explain how the Romans taxed everyone in the countries they occupied, and the taxes were naturally disliked and distrusted. Have a coin to look at and read today's gospel from Matthew 22. Explore the possible responses to the question put to Jesus by the Pharisees and then look at what Jesus managed to say about it in his reply. He is suggesting that the giving to God is in a different "currency" from our civilian duties and loyalties. Our responsibility to God arises from our recognition of his total authority, and our loving response to his gifts to us.

As far as our political and national responsibilities are concerned, we are dealing with other human beings. Loyalty and respect are important, along with the willingness to question injustice and challenge corruption.

Praying

You are worthy, our Lord and God,
to receive glory and honor and power.
For you have created all things,
and by your will they have their being.

Activities

Supply headline stories from the newspapers which show conflict and violence resulting from nationalism, and instances of oppression and injustice where not only the leaders of one country but the historical legacy of empires cause suffering and degradation. There is space on the activity sheet to draw some of these discussions and challenges together.

Discussion starters

1. What is "Caesar's" and what is God's?

2. It is sometimes said that we end up with the leaders we deserve. Do we expect more of our leaders than we are willing to give ourselves?

Notes

AUTHORITY AND POWER

WHO IS REALLY IN CHARGE?

Over everything, and all time, God is in charge. It is only through him that we exist.

WHAT ABOUT WORLD LEADERS?

We are given the responsibility to be stewards of this world. Those who lead nations have a responsibility to lead for the good of the people.

IS THERE ANYTHING WE CAN DO TO CHANGE INJUSTICE AND ABUSE OF POWER?

Pray, and live under God's authority yourself. Stand up for what is right. Protest against what is wrong. Support the victims.

NATIONALISM

INDIVIDUAL SIN

SOCIETY'S SIN

WHERE IS OPPRESSION AND INJUSTICE TO BLAME?

WHERE IS THE PAST MISUSE OF POWER AND AUTHORITY TO BLAME?

YOU ARE WORTHY, OUR LORD AND GOD, TO RECEIVE GLORY AND HONOUR AND POWER.
FOR YOU HAVE CREATED ALL THINGS, AND BY YOUR WILL THEY HAVE THEIR BEING.

PAST   FUTURE

Thirtieth Sunday in Ordinary Time

Thought for the day

We are to love God with our whole being, and love others as much as we love ourselves.

Readings

Exodus 22:20–26
1 Thessalonians 1:5–10
Matthew 22:34–40

Aim: To see how the whole law and teaching of the prophets are summarized in Jesus' words.

Starter

Put some paper cups filled with water on a table and let everyone try and drink from them with their hands behind their backs. It makes you realize how clever we are at training our arms and hands to provide lovingly for our every need.

Teaching

Every day we get our arms to feed and dress us, switch on the television and the toaster, and open doors. That is a caring consideration, or love, that comes as second nature to us. We are told in the Bible that we are to love God, and love our neighbor as we love ourselves.

Start by reading the gospel, Matthew 22:34–40. Notice how Jesus says that on these two commandments hang all the law and the teaching of the prophets. Show them a parcel with this summary on the label. If you unpack this (do so), you are looking at the whole word of God. (There's a Bible inside.)

Did Jesus make this summary, or was he quoting from somewhere in the Old Testament? He was actually quoting from the book of detailed instructions on ritual and practice for the Levite tribe of priests. This is found in the Book of Leviticus.

Why does loving others as we love ourselves incorporate all those other laws? It's because if we showed to others the kind of attentive caring we lavish on ourselves, there would be no lying, stealing, murder, adultery, envy or lack of respect. All those things happen because we are not thinking considerately of the other person or people.

How does the first commandment fit in? As we love God, establishing him as number one in our lives, his love pours out to us, enabling us to love others in this attentive, considerate way.

Praying

Lord, have mercy upon us
and incline our hearts to keep this law.

Activities

The questions on the activity sheet encourage them to look at the pros and cons of a positive summary of the law, rather than loads of specific negatives. There is also a suggestion for a short sketch in which the body attentively cares for its needs and wants.

Discussion starters

1. What advantage is there in a general summary of the law over the detailed rules system?

2. How does this summary of the law affect the way we live?

Notes

JESUS' SUMMARY OF THE LAW

WHAT DID HE SUMMARISE?

The ten commandments. But he said that everything in the whole Law and all the prophets came from this.

WHAT?

Love the Lord your God, with your whole being, and love your neighbor as yourself.

THAT'S NOT MANY RULES.

No, but if you live by those you will be living the best way possible. It's clear, and simple to remember.

THE 10 COMMANDMENTS

1. I am the Lord – no other gods
2. Don't misuse the Lord's name
3. Keep the Sabbath holy
4. Honor your father and mother
5. Do not murder
6. Do not commit adultery
7. Do not steal
8. Do not tell lies or give false testimony
9. Do not covet neighbor's wife
10. Do not want what others have

① LOVE GOD!
② LOVE YOUR NEIGHBOUR AS YOURSELF!

THE ADVANTAGES OF THE SUMMARY

LORD, HAVE MERCY UPON US AND INCLINE OUR HEARTS TO KEEP THIS LAW.

Thirty-first Sunday in Ordinary Time

Thought for the day

Our lives need to reflect our faith; we are not just called to tell the good news but to live it as well.

Readings

Malachi 1:14—2:2, 8–10
1 Thessalonians 2:7–9, 13
Matthew 23:1–12

Aim: To look at the necessity for living our faith and not being hypocritical.

Starter

Play "Cheat." Deal out an equal number of cards to everyone. The aim is to be the first to get rid of all your cards. This is done by laying down cards in numerical order around the circle, using any suit, so that the first person may place (face down) the ace of spades, the second person the two of diamonds and the third the three of hearts. If you haven't got a suitable card, you can pick any of your cards and lie about what it is as you put it down. If you are challenged and found to be cheating, you take both your cards and those of the challenger. If, when challenged, you are found to be correct, the challenger takes yours and their own cards.

Teaching

It isn't only in cards that we cheat. Often in life we pretend things, either to others or to ourselves and to God. Today we are going to look at God's view of this.

Start by reading the passage from Malachi. Like all the other prophets, Malachi was trying to get the people to be honest to the God of truth. If the priests claim to worship the one true living God, they have got to live that out, rather than leading people astray by their teaching and example. God hates this kind of false religion.

Look in contrast at the kind of ministry shown in 1 Thessalonians. What evidence is there here that the leaders were acting out their faith, rather than leading people astray?

Now read today's gospel. Why is Jesus angry at the behavior of the Pharisees? How are they seen as false guides? Notice how it is Jesus' love and compassion for the people that makes him so concerned about the leaders guiding them away from the loving God. That links with the way the Thessalonians have been cared for rather than preached at.

Use the activity sheet to think about the guidelines Jesus gives for all leaders and teachers of the faith.

Praying

Lord, show me the path of life
and fill me with joy
in your presence.

Activities

There is space on the activity sheet to explore Jesus' guidelines for teachers and leaders, and examples of hypocrisy in times past which we can see now but which people didn't recognize at the time. They are encouraged to look at any areas in our own church or society where there are double standards which need addressing.

Discussion starters

1. How can we preach the good news without words?

2. Hypocrisy starts when those who value what is right find the idea of themselves doing wrong abhorrent. Rather than going down that damaging road of self-deceit, what should be done?

Notes

WALK THE TALK

HOW CAN YOU WALK THE TALK?

You can live the way you say you believe in.

SO IF YOU BELIEVE IN GOD IT SHOULD SHOW?

Yes, it should. People should be able to look at the way you live and guess that you must be a Christian.

SUPPOSE WE LIVED IN A WAY WE THINK JESUS WOULD BE HAPPY TO SEE?

That would be excellent.

HE'D WANT TO SEE US LOOKING AFTER ONE ANOTHER'S NEEDS — LOVING ONE ANOTHER, WOULDN'T HE?

Yes. It's no good saying we love God and then hating everybody, or ignoring them.

MATTHEW 23: 1-12 GUIDELINES FOR TEACHERS AND LEADERS

GOOD TEACHERS AND LEADERS SHOULD...

| VERSES 3 & 4 |
| VERSE 5 |
| VERSES 7 & 8 |
| VERSES 9 & 10 |
| VERSES 11 & 12 |

ANY DOUBLE STANDARDS IN OUR OWN CHURCH OR SOCIETY?

LORD, SHOW ME THE PATH OF LIFE, AND FILL ME WITH JOY IN YOUR PRESENCE.

MAKE A LIST OF GUIDELINES BASED ON JESUS' TEACHING!

Thirty-second Sunday in Ordinary Time

Thought for the day

We need to keep ourselves awake and prepared so that the Day of the Lord does not come to us as darkness rather than light.

Readings

Wisdom 6:12–16
1 Thessalonians 4:13–18
Matthew 25:1–13

Aim: To explore the meaning of the parable of the bridesmaids and Jesus' teaching about the Day of the Lord.

Starter

Who can count a minute? One person has a watch or clock, and when they are ready they say, "Go!" Everyone imagines how long a minute is and puts their hand up when they think a full minute has passed. The person checking the watch or clock notes who is closest to real time.

Teaching

Time is quite elastic and drags if you are waiting. Today we are going to look at some bridesmaids who had a long time to wait.

Go straight to the gospel, reading it as a group with different people taking different parts. What is this parable really talking about? What event is the bridegroom's return that the girls are waiting for? (Jesus coming back in glory.) Who are the bridesmaids, waiting for his return to welcome him? (The Church; Christians.) What is Jesus telling us by the bridegroom taking longer to arrive than expected? (The second coming may not be as close as they thought.)

So what does it mean about some of the bridesmaids letting their oil run low so that their lamps are not shining when the bridegroom returns? (As Christians we need to make sure we are keeping ourselves filled with God's Spirit, so that our lives shine with God's love.)

Praying

O thou who camest from above,
the pure celestial fire to impart,
kindle a flame of sacred love
on the mean altar of my heart.
There let it for thy glory burn
with inextinguishable blaze,
and trembling to its source return

in humble prayer and fervent praise.

Activities

On the activity sheet they are looking at the reading from Thessalonians and its implications, and there are references to help them see the significance of oil and fire, together with the traditional practice in weddings at the time, so that they can place the parable in context.

Discussion starters

1. Why is the way of justice and righteousness a better way for a society to be run?

2. How can we ensure that we have enough oil in our lamps for when they are needed?

Notes

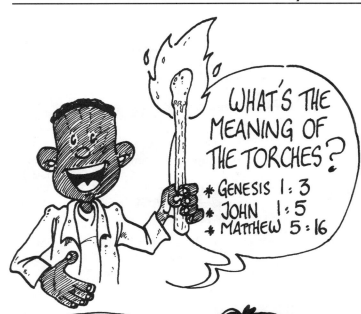

WHAT'S THE MEANING OF THE TORCHES?

* GENESIS 1:3
* JOHN 1:5
* MATTHEW 5:16

WHAT'S THE MEANING OF OIL?

* EXODUS 29:7
* LEVITICUS 8:10, 12
* HEBREWS 1:9
* JAMES 5:14

DON'T MISS OUT!

MISS WHAT?

Miss out on the kingdom of heaven, and all the richness of new life in Christ.

HOW CAN WE BE READY FOR IT?

In today's parable Jesus tells us we need to keep filled up with spiritual 'fuel', so our lives are lit up and shining.

WHERE DOES THE SPIRITUAL FUEL COME FROM?

Whenever we pray, either on our own or together, and whenever we worship, God's Spirit in us grows. Also when we act lovingly.

1 THESSALONIANS 4:13-18

HOW DO WE HAVE HOPE ABOUT OUR LOVED ONES WHO HAVE DIED? (v.14)

WILL WE MISS OUT ON THE LORD'S COMING IN GLORY IF WE HAVE DIED BY THEN? (v.15-17)

YES ☐   NO ☐

O THOU WHO CAMEST FROM ABOVE,
THE PURE CELESTIAL FIRE TO IMPART,
KINDLE A FLAME OF SACRED LOVE
ON THE MEAN ALTAR OF MY HEART.
THERE LET IT FOR THY GLORY BURN
WITH INEXTINGUISHABLE BLAZE,
AND TREMBLING TO ITS SOURCE RETURN
IN HUMBLE PRAYER AND FERVENT PRAISE.

CELESTIAL = FROM HEAVEN
IMPART = GIVE
MEAN = POOR, ORDINARY
INEXTINGUISHABLE = CAN'T PUT IT OUT
FERVENT = ENTHUSIASTIC, KEEN

TRADITIONAL TIMETABLE FOR WEDDING

BRIDE'S FATHER'S HOUSE → THE MARRIAGE

THEN BRIDEGROOM TAKES BRIDE TO HIS OWN HOUSE IN THE EVENING, THEIR WAY LIT BY THE WAITING BRIDESMAIDS.

Thirty-third Sunday in Ordinary Time

Thought for the day

The Day of the Lord will hold terror for the wicked and unprepared, but rejoicing for those living in God's light.

Readings

Proverbs 31:10–13, 19–20, 30–31
1 Thessalonians 5:1–6
Matthew 25:14–30

Aim: To look at the prophesied Day of the Lord, both from the point of view of judgment and mercy.

Starter

Fix a sheet of paper to everyone's backs and provide pens. Everyone goes around writing on the sheets of paper things they appreciate and enjoy about each person. Then the sheets are taken off and given to their owners to read.

Teaching

Read the first part of the passage from 1 Thessalonians and consider why people might be frightened about the end of time (the Day of the Lord).

Now look at the rest of the passage from Thessalonians, where it is still recognized that there will be a Day, a Day of Judgment, but through Jesus there is hope of salvation for us. Jot down the words which describe how we should behave.

Finally read the parable of the talents, with different parts being taken by different people. God wants us to be responsible about the gifts we are entrusted with, and not waste them, hide them, or be too frightened to use them. He wants us to enjoy using them to the full.

Praying

Lord, you have been our dwelling-place
throughout all generations.
Before the mountains were born
or you brought forth the earth and the world,
from everlasting to everlasting
you are God.

(From Psalm 90)

Activities

There are examples on the activity sheet of people who have used their gifts to the glory of God and for the good of the world, and they are encouraged to look at their own gifts and how they could be used to the full in their life.

Discussion starters

1. There are many in our time who assume God is impotent to do either good or evil. In the light of prophecies about the Day of Judgment, should we be so accepting of this, or should it spur us into fervent prayer and urgent action?

2. Has the pendulum swung too far from the "fire and brimstone" terror sermons to the point where we are complacent about the possibility of punishment?

Notes

THE ARTISTS WHO DESIGNED AND MADE THESE STAINED GLASS WINDOWS UPLIFT MANY HEARTS TO WORSHIP.

STAINED GLASS WINDOW AT CHARTRES

GIFTS AND TALENTS

I DON'T THINK I'VE GOT MANY OF THOSE.

We've all been given gifts. Having a gift doesn't mean you've got to be better than anyone else! And there are gifts you might not have realized are gifts.

LIKE WHAT?

Like making people feel comfortable and relaxed; like not giving up easily; like cheering someone up, or listening well.

HOW CAN WE USE THEM BEST?

Keep praying, and keep available. Then God can use those gifts of yours where and when they're most needed.

C.S. LEWIS WROTE ABOUT THE FAITH IN HIS WONDERFUL CHILDREN'S BOOKS.

AS A MEMBER OF PARLIAMENT WILLIAM USED HIS POWERS OF SPEAKING AND WRITING TO GET THE LAWS AGAINST THE SLAVE TRADE CHANGED.

WILLIAM WILBERFORCE

LORD, YOU HAVE BEEN OUR DWELLING-PLACE THROUGHOUT ALL GENERATIONS. BEFORE THE MOUNTAINS WERE BORN OR YOU BROUGHT FORTH THE EARTH AND THE WORLD, FROM EVERLASTING TO EVERLASTING YOU ARE GOD.

(– FROM PSALM 89 –)

HAVE A LOOK AT YOUR OWN GIFTS AND HOW THEY COULD BE USED!

Christ the King

Thought for the day

In total humility, at one with the least of his people, Jesus, the Messiah or Christ, reigns as King, with full authority and honor for eternity.

Readings

Ezekiel 34:11–12, 15–17
1 Corinthians 15:20–26, 28
Matthew 25:31–46

Aim: To look at the nature of Jesus' kingship.

Starter

Have the names and dates of the kings and queens that they know of (King David, King Solomon, Queen of England) written on separate pieces of card and work together to put them in order.

Teaching

Today we are going to look at Jesus as our King, and what kind of King he is.

First look at the passage from Ezekiel, making a note of the image he uses of a shepherd. (Who else was a shepherd who became a king?) This picture fits in well with the Jesus we know from the gospels. (How?)

Look at the passage from 1 Corinthians and notice the images here of power and authority. When was this given to Jesus? After the Resurrection, once sin and death were conquered.

Then read the parable of the sheep and goats. Before you read it together, explain that "all the nations" uses a word referring to those who do not know of Jesus and have not yet heard of him. Share the different parts in the reading. Notice how the second group had not actively done anything wrong but had failed to do active good.

Praying

Come, let us bow down in worship,
let us kneel before the Lord our Maker;
for he is our God
and we are the people of his pasture,
the flock under his care.

(From Psalm 95)

Activities

The activity sheet further explores the kingship of Jesus as a servant, full of humility. And there is a wordsearch of the different titles of Jesus from different references, for which they will need a Bible.

Discussion starters

1. What does today's gospel say to those who claim that they have never done anyone any harm?

2. If we are to be in nature like the Christ, how do today's readings suggest we should be living?

Notes

CHRIST IS THE KING

WHAT KIND OF KING IS JESUS?

The ideas of authority and power are there. But Jesus' greatness is not shown in wealth or force, but humanity and love.

LIKE A SHEPHERD KING?

Yes, that's it. He searches for the lost and binds up the broken like a shepherd.

WHAT ABOUT A SERVANT?

Yes, Jesus' role as king is washing our feet. It's quite an amazing humility.

TITLES OF JESUS

D	M	S	L	E	U	N	A	M	M	E	J
O	E	N	T	C	P	R	O	D	L	N	O
F	L	Q	S	L	R	U	Z	A	S	E	I
R	A	Z	B	O	I	P	T	C	M	P	K
N	M	V	K	P	N	S	Q	N	S	V	B
J	B	Q	S	K	C	O	C	B	A	Q	T
L	O	R	D	S	E	D	F	F	V	F	M
I	F	R	O	N	O	G	E	G	I	Y	J
J	G	A	P	A	F	N	W	I	O	L	G
M	O	D	U	E	P	W	O	V	U	D	K
H	D	A	N	R	E	V	R	F	R	R	D
A	S	I	C	F	A	T	D	H	M	F	H
Z	R	B	J	Y	C	U	G	T	E	A	C
P	L	X	Z	M	E	S	S	I	A	H	N

IS THIS OUR KING?

SO WHAT DOES THAT MEAN FOR US?

JOHN 13 : 13-17

COME, LET US BOW DOWN IN WORSHIP, LET US KNEEL BEFORE THE LORD OUR MAKER; FOR HE IS OUR GOD AND WE ARE THE PEOPLE OF HIS PASTURE, THE FLOCK UNDER HIS CARE. (—FROM PSALM 94—)

Isaiah 9:6 _ _ _ _ _ _ / _ _ / _ _ _ _   John 1:29 _ _ _ _ / _ _ / _ _ _

John 4:25-26 _ _ _ _ _ _ _   Matthew 1:23 _ _ _ _ _ _ _ _

John 1:34 _ _ _ / _ _ / _ _ _   Luke 2:11 _ _ _ _

Matthew 12:40 _ _ _ / _ _ / _ _ _   John 1:14 _ _ _ _

Special Feasts

Mary, Mother of God—January 1

Thought for the day
Jesus Christ, the Son of God, is born of a woman.

Readings
Numbers 6:22–27
Galatians 4:4–7
Luke 2:16–21

Aim: To appreciate Mary's special calling as the mother of Christ.

Starter
Choose a trustworthy and sensible person and take them aside. Tell them to try and convince the others that they have won a thousand dollars. Back in the group, this person says they have won a thousand dollars, and weathers the scorn and disbelief, sticking to their story. Have a show of hands as to who is convinced and who isn't, and ask the "prize winner" how it felt to be disbelieved and thought of as a liar. Today we are looking at Mary's special calling to be the mother of Christ, and some of the problems it must have caused for her.

Teaching
As part of our celebration of Christmas we are celebrating Mary's willingness to cooperate with God in his saving work by becoming the mother of Christ. Read together the passage from Numbers, remembering how Gabriel had greeted Mary at the Annunciation, calling her "blessed among women." Mary, in her humility, knew her need of God and so was open to his will, ready to be used in bringing Life itself to birth as a human baby.

Read the passage from Galatians, drawing attention to the need for the Son of God to enter into the full experience of being human and Jewish, in order to do the work of redeeming from the "inside." Also, since through Jesus we are made children and heirs, in a spiritual sense we share with Jesus Mary's mothering. Her calling to be his mother extends to being, in that spiritual sense, the mother of the Church, in every generation.

Now read today's gospel, noticing how Mary, this young mother given such a great responsibility, absorbs everything and treasures it all in her heart. She is still open to God and his meaning, still attentive to hear what he is saying in all the events of her baby's birth. It is that openness and attentive listening to God which makes it possible for God to use her for such an important role. She never draws attention to herself or tries to bask in Jesus' glory, but always directs our attention to Jesus Christ, her Lord and her Son.

Praying
Father, we give you thanks
for the openness and willingness of Mary
to do your will
and take on the mothering of your Son.
We ask that her prayers may direct us
to attentive listening and openness to you,
so that with Mary we may say:
"Let it be to me according to your word."

Activities
There are examples on the activity sheet of people who have experienced Mary directing them to Jesus Christ, her Son, and some questions to encourage them to think seriously about their own calling in life and their openness to God.

Discussion starters
1. Why was it so important for the Savior to come into the world as a human baby, born of a woman?

2. How can Mary's example of carrying, bearing and parenting the Christ help us in our own relationship with Christ?

Notes

The Presentation of the Lord (Candlemas)– February 2

Thought for the day

In accordance with Jewish tradition, the Light of the World is presented as a first-born baby in the temple at Jerusalem.

Readings

Malachi 3:1–4
Hebrews 2:14–18
Luke 2:22–40

Aim: To see how Simeon and Anna's faithfulness and trust were rewarded, and relate this to our own faith.

Starter

Play a trust game, such as making a close circle around one person who allows themselves to fall in any direction. The circle of people around them prevents them from getting anywhere near the ground. Today we are looking at two people who knew they could really trust God.

Teaching

Read the gospel passage together, with different people taking the parts of Simeon and Anna. Using the format provided on the activity sheet, discuss *who* was involved, *what* happened, *where* it happened, *when* and *why*. Draw out the fact that both Simeon and Anna had been faithful in prayer for many years, so that they were able to recognize what God was saying to them, and trust him to do what he said. They had also learned to be obedient. (Suppose Simeon had decided not to act on God's nudging to go to the temple that day.)

On a sheet of paper, write in the middle: "What about us?" Around this question jot down what Simeon and Anna can teach us about good practice in our own lives. (This may include such things as the value of regular daily prayer, getting to know what the Bible says, listening to God as well as talking to him, doing what God asks straight away, trusting God, being patient, being prepared for God to answer our prayers in unexpected ways.)

Praying

Use the activity sheet you have completed and go around the ideas, asking God to help us grow in each of these areas.

Activities

Give each person one of the ideas to express in mime and present this with a reader as part of the service. Alternatively, write and illustrate each point and make a display for the church titled "Learning from Simeon and Anna."

Discussion starters

1. Why was it necessary for Christ to become one with the human race and with the faithful remnant of Israel in order to save the world?

2. How was Simeon able to recognize this particular baby as the Christ? Do we expect God to tell us things?

Notes

HAVE A LOOK AT LUKE 2 v. 22 - 40

WHO?

WHAT?

WHERE?

WHEN?

WHY?

READ EXODUS 13 v. 2, 12

SIMEON AND ANNA

WHO WERE THEY? They were elderly, faithful people who had loved God all their lives.

WHAT DID GOD TELL THEM?
He showed them that Jesus was the Messiah, or Savior, who the people had been waiting for over the centuries. He also put into Simeon's mind something to tell Mary.

WHAT WAS THAT? Jesus would be a sign that some would accept gladly and others would reject. Jesus would help people see their true selves and help them put right anything wrong in their lives. Jesus was coming as Savior not just for the Jewish people but the non-Jewish (Gentiles) as well.

HOW DID THEY RECOGNISE JESUS?
They were used to noticing God speaking into their hearts. God told them and they listened.

WHY DID JOSEPH AND MARY BRING THESE TWO ALONG TO THE TEMPLE?

THIS WEEK'S PRAYER IS SIMEON'S AS WELL!

LORD NOW YOU LET YOUR SERVANT GO IN PEACE: YOUR WORD HAS BEEN FULFILLED.
MY OWN EYES HAVE SEEN THE SALVATION: WHICH YOU HAVE PREPARED IN THE SIGHT OF EVERY PEOPLE;
A LIGHT TO REVEAL YOU TO THE NATIONS: AND THE GLORY OF YOUR PEOPLE ISRAEL.

Saint John the Baptist— June 24

Thought for the day

John is born with a mission to prepare the way for the Messiah by calling people to repentance.

Readings

Isaiah 49:1–6
Acts 13:22–26
Luke 1:57–66, 80

Aim: To see how the coming of John the Baptist was essential preparation for the coming of the Messiah.

Starter

Melt some chocolate and pour it into little molds, or coat things with it, such as cookies, marzipan or fruit. Leave to dry on wax paper or foil.

Teaching

We couldn't have made these delicious things unless we had prepared the chocolate by melting it to make it flexible. Today we are celebrating the birth of John the Baptist, who urged people to prepare their lives, so they would be ready to receive the Messiah when he came. Like our chocolate, they needed God to soften them and make them warm and responsive to his love, so they could be made new.

Read the passage from Isaiah, where the chosen people are called to be the light of the nations, so that God's salvation may reach to the ends of the earth. Pick up on this expectation and collective calling, and the hope of the Messiah.

Now read Luke 1:5–25, followed by today's gospel, to get the full picture of the circumstances surrounding the birth of John the Baptist. Although this is quite a lot of reading, it is sometimes valuable to look at a complete section of a narrative like this. It makes clear that the prophecies are being fulfilled, and the pace has quickened; there is an urgency of preparation like the "Scramble!" command or the red alert which gets everyone suddenly extra attentive and poised. God is about to come among his people and John will be the one to announce God's coming.

We are all important "members" of Christ's Body, the Church. When we are "tuned in" to God he can work with us and through us, and we are the only ones who can do the particular work God needs us to do.

Praying

O Lord, you search me out and you know me,
you know my resting and my rising,
you mark when I walk or lie down,
all my ways lie open to you.
For it was you who created my being,
knit me together in my mother's womb.
I thank you for the wonder of my being,
for the wonders of all your creation.

(From Psalm 139)

Activities

On the activity sheet there is a John the Baptist fact-file to complete, and an opportunity to explore their own area of calling and work within their life situation at the moment.

Discussion starters

1. Why did Zechariah lose his power of speech until the naming of John?

2. In what way is John the Baptist like the prophet Elijah?

Notes

NAME : JOHN, KNOWN AS
'_____'

FATHER'S NAME : _____

MOTHER'S NAME : _____

AGE BAND OF PARENTS

☐ YOUNG   ☐ MIDDLE AGED   ☐ ELDERLY

MISSION : _____
_____

UNUSUAL CIRCUMSTANCES OF BIRTH : _____
_____
_____

THE VOICE OF ONE CRYING IN THE WILDERNESS

WAS JOHN RELATED TO JESUS?

Yes. Mary and John's mother, Elizabeth, were cousins.

WHY WAS A MESSENGER NEEDED?

People need to be prepared for important changes. If they were to be ready to hear Jesus and recognize him, they needed to be right with God first.

HOW DID JOHN DO THAT?

He helped them see where their lives needed sorting out, and 'washing'. As forgiven people, full of love for God, they were more likely to recognize who Jesus was.

WHERE ARE WE CALLED TO WORK WITH GOD?

AND HOW?

AT HOME

IN HOBBIES...

AT SCHOOL

...AND SPORTS

O LORD, YOU SEARCH ME OUT AND YOU KNOW ME,
YOU KNOW MY RESTING AND MY RISING,
YOU MARK WHEN I WALK OR LIE DOWN,
ALL MY WAYS LIE OPEN TO YOU.
FOR IT WAS YOU WHO CREATED MY BEING,
KNIT ME TOGETHER IN MY MOTHER'S WOMB.
I THANK YOU FOR THE WONDER OF MY
                                    BEING,
FOR THE WONDERS OF ALL YOUR CREATION.
        (– FROM PSALM 139 –)

Saints Peter and Paul— June 29

Thought for the day

Through the dedication of the apostles Peter and Paul, the gospel of Jesus Christ spread and the Church was rapidly established.

Readings

Acts 12:1–11
2 Timothy 4:6–8, 17–18
Matthew 16:13–19

Aim: To look at how the ministries of Peter and Paul balanced and complemented each other in the early Church.

Starter

Provide a varied assortment of objects, a broom handle, string and two matching containers. The task is to fill the containers with varied loads which exactly balance each other.

Teaching

We have just seen how very different things can balance each other, and today we are looking at the very different ministries of Peter and Paul and how they balanced each other so that God's plan for the early Church was accomplished.

Have two large outlined drawings, one of Peter and one of Paul, with their names underneath. Collect from discussion any facts or characteristics they know about Paul and Peter already, and write these on the spaces. Add to these so that you include the following information:

Peter

• Placed in charge of the early Church

• Ministry to the faithful Jewish people

• Martyr

Paul

• Preacher, teacher and letter writer

• Spreading good news to the Gentiles

• Martyr

Now read today's gospel, followed by the passage from Acts 12. Draw attention to the way Peter's commission (Matthew 16) was showing up in his behavior and trust in God (Acts 12). You could also look up the references on the activity sheet.

Now look at the reading from 2 Timothy, and use some of the references on the activity sheet to pick up on what experiences had led up to Paul claiming that the Lord has stood at his side and given him strength.

Praying

Loving Father, as members of your Church
we offer ourselves for your work
in this generation.
Make us strong in faith
and happy to give ourselves away
in serving you.

Activities

On the activity sheet there are Peter and Paul profiles with Identi-Kit characteristics to build up on each. These include mistakes and weaknesses, and the way God can use and transform all our faults as well as our strengths, as long as we open up to his life-giving Spirit.

Discussion starters

1. How did the twin ministries of Peter and Paul complement each other?

2. What can we learn from Peter and Paul's adventures and letters about effective evangelization?

Notes

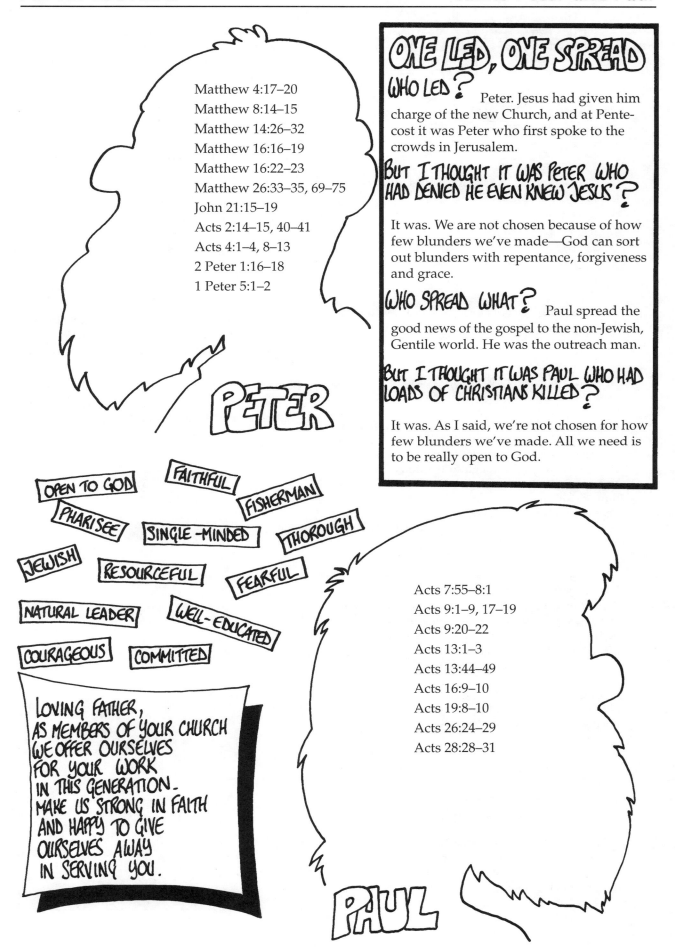

Matthew 4:17–20
Matthew 8:14–15
Matthew 14:26–32
Matthew 16:16–19
Matthew 16:22–23
Matthew 26:33–35, 69–75
John 21:15–19
Acts 2:14–15, 40–41
Acts 4:1–4, 8–13
2 Peter 1:16–18
1 Peter 5:1–2

PETER

ONE LED, ONE SPREAD

WHO LED? Peter. Jesus had given him charge of the new Church, and at Pentecost it was Peter who first spoke to the crowds in Jerusalem.

BUT I THOUGHT IT WAS PETER WHO HAD DENIED HE EVEN KNEW JESUS?

It was. We are not chosen because of how few blunders we've made—God can sort out blunders with repentance, forgiveness and grace.

WHO SPREAD WHAT? Paul spread the good news of the gospel to the non-Jewish, Gentile world. He was the outreach man.

BUT I THOUGHT IT WAS PAUL WHO HAD LOADS OF CHRISTIANS KILLED?

It was. As I said, we're not chosen for how few blunders we've made. All we need is to be really open to God.

OPEN TO GOD   FAITHFUL   FISHERMAN
PHARISEE   SINGLE-MINDED   THOROUGH
JEWISH   RESOURCEFUL   FEARFUL
NATURAL LEADER   WELL-EDUCATED
COURAGEOUS   COMMITTED

LOVING FATHER,
AS MEMBERS OF YOUR CHURCH
WE OFFER OURSELVES
FOR YOUR WORK
IN THIS GENERATION.
MAKE US STRONG IN FAITH
AND HAPPY TO GIVE
OURSELVES AWAY
IN SERVING YOU.

Acts 7:55–8:1
Acts 9:1–9, 17–19
Acts 9:20–22
Acts 13:1–3
Acts 13:44–49
Acts 16:9–10
Acts 19:8–10
Acts 26:24–29
Acts 28:28–31

PAUL

The Transfiguration of the Lord— August 6

Jesus is seen in all God's glory, and as fulfilling the Law and the prophets.

Readings
Daniel 7:9–10, 13–14
2 Peter 1:16–19
Matthew 17:1–9

Aim: To look at God's revealed glory in the Transfiguration and his glory in our world.

Starter
Give out some candy which have centers different from the outside. People may be able to guess what they taste like because they've eaten other ones that look very similar. But the only way to know what this particular candy is really like, through and through, is to eat it, very slowly, noticing the way it changes as you get through to the different layers, and paying attention to the different textures throughout the experience. (The candy are now savored, with people jotting down any words that describe the different experiences of texture, flavor and so on.)

Teaching
Usually we tend to rush through even pleasant things like eating candy, without really appreciating them, and it's a good idea to give these ordinary things our full attention sometimes, as we can use all these little things to give us glimpses of God's glory, as well as the more dramatic things.

Today, as we celebrate God's glory being revealed in Jesus at the Transfiguration, we are also reminded of the way the whole of earth, as well as heaven, is filled with glory, if we have our senses open to notice.

Read the passage from Daniel, where he is trying to describe the full glory of heaven in human language. Even though this is pretty much impossible, the passage does set off in our minds some sense of that brightness and majesty of a totally loving and powerful God.

Now read the account of the Transfiguration from the gospel, so that they can see how it is like seeing the glory of heaven but on the earth, in Jesus. What does that tell us about Jesus' identity? Look at what the voice of God is heard to proclaim. How did the experience make the disciples feel (a) immediately (b) at the events of the Crucifixion and Resurrection?

Read the letter from Peter to see how the amazing experience had stayed in his mind right through to the early Church.

Praying
The Lord is king, let earth rejoice,
let all the coastlands be glad.
Cloud and darkness are his clothing;
his throne, majesty and might.
For you indeed are the Lord,
most high above the earth,
exalted far above all spirits.

(From Psalm 97)

Activities
Give out large sheets of paper (lengths of wallpaper, perhaps) and sponges to paint with so that they can express the glory of the living God on a large scale.

Discussion starters
1. How would the Transfiguration strengthen the disciples for the scandal of the cross?

2. Is transfiguration something that happens, to some extent, in all who pray?

Notes

HEAVEN AND EARTH ARE FULL OF YOUR GLORY!

GOD'S GLORY

WHY WERE THE DISCIPLES FRIGHTENED BY GOD'S GLORY?

We have no idea of how it must be to glimpse the power and glory of God, like they did. Most of the time we think of God as much like us, but they saw his real greatness and it shocked and scared them.

WHY WAS JESUS TALKING WITH MOSES AND ELIJAH?

Moses represents the Law, and Elijah the prophets, so God was showing the disciples that Jesus was fulfilling the Old Testament, and had authority.

THAT MUST HAVE HELPED THE DISCIPLES SEE WHO JESUS WAS.

Yes, and it must have helped them understand the crucifixion.

DO WE TAKE GOD'S GLORY FOR GRANTED?

DO WE IGNORE IT MOST OF THE TIME?

THE LORD IS KING,
LET EARTH REJOICE,
LET ALL THE COASTLANDS BE GLAD.
CLOUD AND DARKNESS ARE HIS CLOTHING;
HIS THRONE, MAJESTY AND MIGHT.
FOR YOU INDEED ARE THE LORD,
MOST HIGH ABOVE THE EARTH,
EXALTED FAR ABOVE ALL SPIRITS.

(– FROM PSALM 96 –)

IDEAS FOR A LARGE-SCALE IMPRESSION OF THE GLORY OF THE LIVING GOD.

The Assumption— August 15

Thought for the day
The Almighty has done great things for me!

Readings
Revelation 11:19; 12:1–6, 10
1 Corinthians 15:20–27
Luke 1:39–56

Aim: To know the hope of resurrection as we celebrate the assumption of Mary.

Starter
Have a picture of Mary, cut into wet mud or clay on a board, and a selection of small leaves and flower petals of different colors. They press the petals lightly into the wet clay to complete the picture.

Teaching
Today we celebrate Mary being taken into the glory of heaven; it is a wonderful celebration both of Mary's openness to God's will and of the great hope of full resurrection for everyone who believes in the risen Christ.

Begin by reading today's gospel, where Mary is greeted by her cousin Elizabeth as the mother of her Lord, and which includes the Magnificat— Mary's song of praise and joy which traces God's promise of salvation and his faithfulness. Next look at the passage from 1 Corinthians, where Paul is celebrating the great Christian hope of resurrection, shown and promised by the Resurrection of Jesus Christ in his victory over death. Paul is looking both at the new life we live in Christ here and now, and also at the hope of that time of fulfillment and accomplishment at the end of time, when all the faithful will be gathered and, made perfect, live in the full glory of heaven forever.

Finally read the passage from Revelation together. In Mary we have a wonderful example of what openness to God's will can do. In the Christly love she pours out we have a picture of the Church being filled with the love of God and pouring it out in loving service for the good of the world. We look forward today to that resurrection promise for which our receptive openness and commitment are the only necessary qualifications, since it is God's good grace which saves us.

Praying
Hail, Mary, full of grace,
the Lord is with thee:
blessed art thou among women,
and blessed is the fruit of thy womb, Jesus.
Holy Mary, Mother of God,
pray for us sinners now,
and at the hour of our death. Amen.

Activities
On the activity sheet there are different aspects of Mary's openness and commitment which encourage us in our spiritual journey. Any suggestions for loving outreach which come from today's discussion can be noted and put into action by the parish or in the neighborhood.

Discussion starters
1. What holds us back from total self-giving?

2. If the Church is to be truly the Body of Christ, what do we need to learn from the life and example of Our Lady?

Notes

FOLLOWING MARY'S EXAMPLE...

LET IT BE FOR ME AS GOD WANTS

MARY ENCOURAGES US TO...

... EVEN WHEN THAT'S NOT THE COOLEST JOB

MARY ENCOURAGES US TO...

DO WHAT MY SON TELLS YOU

MARY ENCOURAGES US TO...

DON'T RUN AWAY FROM PAIN AND SUFFERING

MARY ENCOURAGES US TO...

IN OUR PARISH WE COULD FOLLOW MARY'S EXAMPLE BY ...

HAIL, MARY, FULL OF GRACE,
THE LORD IS WITH THEE;
BLESSED ART THOU AMONG WOMEN,
AND BLESSED IS THE FRUIT OF THY WOMB, JESUS.
HOLY MARY, MOTHER OF GOD,
PRAY FOR US SINNERS NOW,
AND AT THE HOUR OF OUR DEATH. AMEN.

MARY IS IN HEAVEN

WHY IS MARY HONOURED ABOVE ALL THE OTHER SAINTS?

Because her role was, and is, such a special one. God chose her to be the mother of our Savior, Jesus Christ. To have the Son of God growing in you, and in your care as parent, is closeness to God which no one else has.

WHAT CAN WE LEARN FROM MARY?

Love and devotion to Christ, openness to God and the willingness to work with God, even if that hurts.

WHY IS THIS,

IN OUR THOUGHTS TODAY?

WHAT DOES IT TELL US ABOUT THIS?

The Triumph of The Holy Cross— September 14

Thought for the day

Through Christ's loving obedience, even to death on a cross, he has opened up the way for us to eternal life.

Readings

Numbers 21:4–9
Philippians 2:6–11
John 3:13–17

Aim: To explore the triumph of the cross.

Starter

Have some magnifying glasses or a microscope to look at things, noticing the things that are hidden until you look at them this closely.

Teaching

Our faith is about deep and holy things, so we'd expect some of these to be full of mystery. As humans contemplating the all-powerful God, there are bound to be some things our minds can't grasp. Some things we sense and "know," rather than being able to set out as clear evidence. Thinking of the cross as a triumph is quite a mystery, but the mystery draws us deeper into the mind and heart of God.

First read the passage from Numbers, where the bronze snake is lifted up by God's friend Moses, so that all those who are dying from snake bites may draw healing and life from looking at it. How is that rather like a picture of Jesus on the cross? Those who are mortal, and know their need of healing, can gaze at the Christ, dying out of love for us, and find there peace and healing and new life.

Read today's gospel next, linking the Old Testament passage and having everybody reading John 3:16. Notice that there is no sense of Jesus coming to condemn, but to save us. Read the Philippians passage to see how Paul sees Jesus' mission, and notice the total self-emptying, humility and obedience to God's loving will.

Having read these passages, use the activity sheet to record in what ways the cross stood for failure, and in what ways for victory. Help them to see that the failure and degrading nature of the Crucifixion were all part of the self-giving love which triumphs over evil and death.

Praying

Alleluia, sing to Jesus,
his the scepter, his the throne;
alleluia, his the triumph,
his the victory alone.
Hark, the songs of peaceful Sion
thunder like a mighty flood;
Jesus, out of every nation,
hath redeemed us by his blood.

Activities

On the activity sheet they can tease out some of the reasons we see the cross as the supreme victory, even as we recognize its failure and degradation. There is also a cross to complete with the aid of Bible references.

Discussion starters

1. How can the horror of an innocent young man being crucified be counted as "triumph?"

2. What can we learn from the cross that will help us when faced with the problem of suffering?

Notes

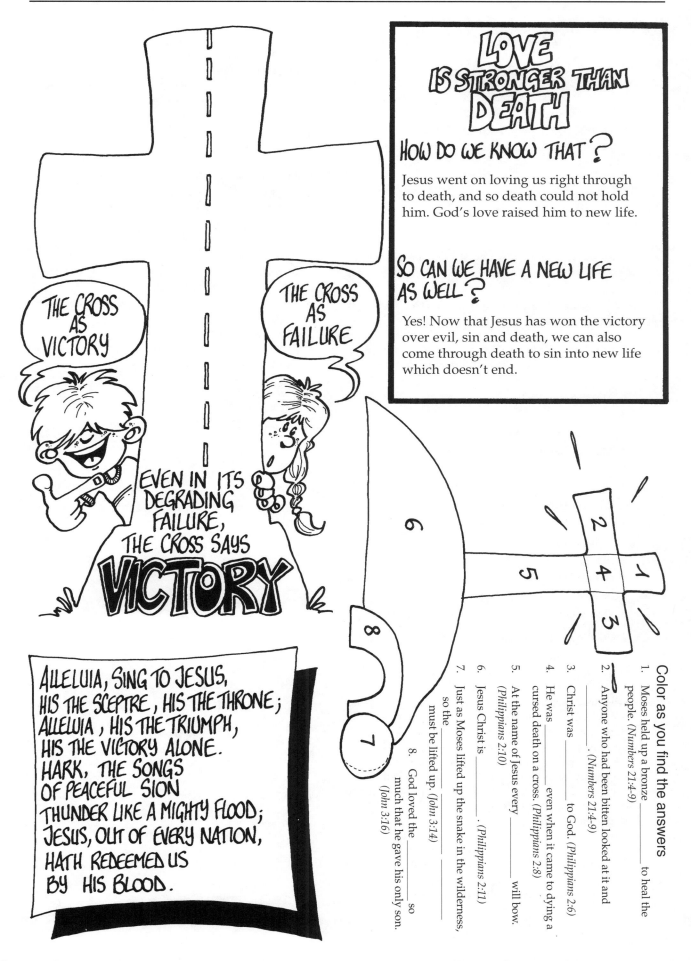

All Saints— November 1

Thought for the day

Lives that have shone with God's love on earth are filled with joy as they see their Lord face to face.

Readings

Revelation 7:2–4, 9–14
1 John 3:1–3
Matthew 5:1–12

Aim: To explore sanctity and the heavenly reward.

Starter

Provide each group with a diary which gives saints days, together with a book of saints to use as a reference book. Give each group a list of dates, and they have to discover whose saint's days these are, and what each saint is remembered for. Here are some dates to choose from:

- March 1: Saint David
- March 17: Saint Patrick
- April 23: Saint George
- May 19: Saint Dunstan
- June 9: Saint Columba
- June 22: Saint Alban
- August 11: Saint Clare
- August 27: Saint Monica
- October 4: Saint Francis
- November 11: Saint Martin
- November 16: Saint Margaret, Queen of Scotland
- November 30: Saint Andrew
- December 6: Saint Nicholas

Then they can tell one another what they've discovered.

Teaching

All through the year we celebrate the saints, and today we remember all of them, together with all those unknown to us but known to God for their special friendship. What is saintliness? Is it a demure, holy expression on a painting or in a stained-glass window? The readings for All Saints show us that these are ordinary people, made extraordinary by their openness to God and their dependence on him.

Read the gospel passage. These "Beatitudes" or the "blesseds" are aptly named, since they do stress the natural happy outcome of living in the way of God's love. It is knowing our need of God that opens us up to receive all the gifts he longs to give us. The Beatitudes are like the saintly handbook, and in the Psalm we do some saint-spotting too.

1 John 3:1–3 looks forward to the hope which is seen in the vision of Revelation, chapter 7. Explain the difficulties of expressing heaven in images of time and human experience, and list the qualities of heaven that this passage hints at.

Praying

Amen!
Praise and glory
and wisdom and thanks and honor
and power and strength
be to our God forever and ever. Amen!

Activities

The prayer is set out on the activity sheet with space to illustrate the joy and peace of heaven, and they are encouraged to think about what a saint is.

Discussion starters

1. What factors prevent us knowing our need of God?

2. What prevents us from trusting God with our deepest needs?

Notes

MONICA – MOTHER OF SAINT AUGUSTINE

Date: 4th century
Saintliness: Lived with violent and unfaithful husband and mother-in-law, but kept faith and prayed for them all. Husband became a Christian a year before he died. Son was a pain, too, but she kept on praying for him and look what happened!

SAINTS

WHAT MAKES A SAINT?

Saints are ordinary people. They are made extraordinary by their openness to God and their dependence on him.

IS THAT MORE IMPORTANT THAN THE THINGS THEY DO?

Well, the good things happen naturally, as a result of where they are with God.

SO YOU CAN'T PRETEND BY DOING LOTS OF STUFF TO LOOK GOOD?

No! You have to get it in the right order – get close to God and all the rest follows.

CAN ANYONE BECOME A SAINT?

Yes. There's no age limit or IQ requirement.

BISHOP NICHOLAS (SANTA CLAUS)

Date: 4th century
Place: Turkey
Saintliness: Imprisoned during persecution. Very generous and kind. Gave marriage dowries in gold to three girls who would otherwise have been forced into living by prostitution.

COLUMBA OF IONA

Date: 6th century
Place: Came from Ireland to Scotland and England
Saintliness: He opened his whole life to God's leading, and it took him on many journeys, telling people about Jesus and giving them new hope.

HOW DO YOU THINK OF HEAVEN?

AMEN! PRAISE AND GLORY AND WISDOM AND THANKS AND HONOUR AND POWER AND STRENGTH BE TO OUR GOD FOR EVER AND EVER AMEN!

Feasts of the Dedication of a Church

Thought for the day

The church building symbolizes the spiritual temple, being built of the living stones of God's people.

Readings

2 Chronicles 5:6–11, 13—6:2 or Acts 7:44–50
1 Corinthians 3:9–13, 16–17
John 4:19–24

Aim: To look at what it means for the transcendent God to dwell in a building.

Starter

Set a timer for two minutes and ask everyone to write down the names of all the people they know, the towns and countries they have visited, and the subjects they have had lessons in at school. When the two minutes are up, ask them to look over their own lists. That represents just two minutes of thinking, and if the room could now be filled with all the people and places mentioned there, it would be pretty crowded. Each of us holds a huge landscape of places and people inside our heads.

Teaching

We have seen how we are really far bigger than we look. Today, as we celebrate the dedication of our church, we are thinking about how the great God of earth and heaven can dwell in a church building. Of course, our God is far too great to be contained in a building, because both heaven and earth are full of his glory, and all that exists is contained in God, the source of all creation. But, rather like all the ideas, memories and knowledge we have in our minds, God's presence dwells in the church building dedicated to him, where daily prayer and offering make it hallowed as a meeting place for God and his gathered people.

Read the passage from 2 Chronicles or Acts, which recognizes both God's transcendent greatness and his closeness and humility; our God travels with his people and stands among them where they are. (How does that link up with the Christmas story?)

Now read the gospel, looking for any guidelines Jesus is giving us for how we should be worshipping God. What does it mean to worship in spirit and in truth? Do we do this? How does our church building help us to do it?

Praying

Father, in this holy place
we sense your presence with us.
Build us up like a strong building,
firm in faith and ready to be used.

Activities

There are different parts of the church building to label and write in their value, and there is also space for looking at how the church building is used for God's work.

Discussion starters

1. What do you particularly thank God for on this anniversary of your church's dedication?

2. What are the advantages for a community of having particular buildings dedicated to God?

Notes

THE HOUSE OF GOD

GOD CAN'T LIVE IN A BUILDING, CAN HE?

No, God is far too great and glorious to be 'contained' anywhere. The whole of creation is held within the mind of God.

SO HOW IS A CHURCH GOD'S HOUSE?

We set a building apart specially to worship God and to be a place of prayer.

IS THAT WHY IT FEELS 'HOLY'?

Yes, the prayer and worship of your church fills this space with God's peace and love.

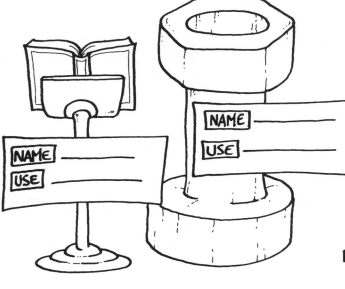

HOW IS YOUR CHURCH BUILDING USED FOR GOD'S WORK?

OUR CHURCH IS USED LIKE THIS ...

FATHER,
IN THIS HOLY PLACE
WE SENSE YOUR PRESENCE
WITH US.
BUILD US UP LIKE
A STRONG BUILDING,
FIRM IN FAITH
AND READY TO BE USED.